A Dagg
at
my Table

A Dagg at my Table

John Clarke

Writings 1977-1996

Hodder Moa Beckett

Dedication

This book is dedicated to the memory of Richard Priest,
a gifted and loving friend.

ISBN 1-86958-316-7

© 1996 Roderick Willows Pty Ltd

Illustrations: Jenny Coopes

First published 1996
Reprinted 1996
Reprinted 1997

Published in 1996 by Hodder Moa Beckett Publishers Limited
[a member of the Hodder Headline Group]
4 Whetu Place, Mairangi Bay, Auckland, New Zealand

Printed by Wright & Carman (NZ) Ltd, Upper Hutt, New Zealand

Contents

Introduction

Many older readers will recall an earlier time in New Zealand, a vivid and exhilarating time when a young nation, poised on the threshold of greatness, called forth from its ranks a natural leader.

From the starkly beautiful central North Island, erosion capital of the world and home of the Raurimu Spiral, came a figure uniquely attuned to the hour. No problem was too great, no matter so Byzantine in its complexity that he could not cut to its heart. He was fair-minded in all things, graceful under pressure and was capable of developing strong opinions unspoilt by knowledge or formal logic. He specialised in the common sense solution and the self-evident truth, and his language was that of Arnold, of Herbert and of Trevor.

His name was Frederick, of the House of Dagg. Born many years earlier, for reasons which need not trouble us here, he had undergone a comprehensive training in all aspects of farmwork and had then attended school from the age of five. His schooling was typical of its time and extremely effective in every way. The New Zealand Education Department had set rigorous standards. Fred learnt that the angles outside parallel lines were equal to the opposite ones inside the lines. He learnt the French for 'big absorbant bathtowel'. By the age of 17 he knew the valency of carbon and the German for 'I have fallen in love with the exit to the static air-display.' These skills have not been required nearly as often as the Department led him to believe but there is still time and, should the need ever arise, Fred and a whole generation of New Zealanders will be able to calculate the compound interest on the square root of x, or the use of irony by Jane Austen, whichever is the lesser, and discuss its impact on the Chartist Movement. (30 marks).

As he obtained to the estate of adulthood, Fred was already instinctively grappling with important issues of nationhood and philosophy. He supported the dropping of superphosphate on farms because he had a brother-in-law with a dung-dusting concern up the Pohangina Valley, but he was troubled by the realisation that the cobalt in the soil of the volcanic plateau was building up to a point where they would soon have to drop soil on it to prevent it from becoming a cobalt deposit.

Matters came to a head when Fred received a letter from his friend Bruce Bayliss, who was at that time a seasonal mutton-birder on Stewart Island. Bruce was not a man given to display but it was obvious that he had a problem. There was no work on the island and Bruce was obliged to pick up the unemployment benefit, which at that time was $137. There was no unemployment officer on Stewart Island and in order to obtain the benefit Bruce caught the boat to Bluff, travelled by bus to Invercargill, collected the emolument and arranged lodgings for the night since the next bus back to Bluff did not leave until the following morning. The next day he caught the boat at Bluff and arrived home in the middle of the afternoon. The total cost of this exercise was $138.

Bruce wrote a letter to the Department. The problem with collecting the assistance, he pointed out, was that it was not commercially viable. The Department replied that Bruce was the victim of an anomaly in the system. They thanked him for calling it to their attention. The reason there was no unemployment office on Stewart Island, they explained, was that for some time there had been no unemployment there. But since he was now unemployed and since he lived there, would he care to become the unemployment officer for the island? Bruce accepted the post and was sent a box of forms which were to be filled in each month, the top form to be sent to Wellington, the office copy to be filed alphabetically and cross-referenced as to date. At the end of the first month, Bruce sent off his first report stating that, since he was employed, there was now no unemployment on Stewart Island. As a result of this, the Department sacked him.

Fred decided at this point it was time to clear his throat and deliver himself of a few opinions. This book contains some of them. They wouldn't all fit.

Radio Scripts

1977-1981

During the late 1970s and early 1980s, Mr Dagg graciously consented to broadcast regularly on radio on matters of the utmost importance ranging from the general character of the human experience to the offering of helpful hints to those entrusted with the care and governance of the nation and its economy. His broadcasts were extremely valuable in every way although ultimately, of course, those entrusted with governance worked out what he was saying and he was stopped.

CAREERS

One of the significant services provided during these radio years was that of the Fred Dagg Careers Advisory Bureau. Its work was broad in its scope and has proved to be of lasting value. It has never been more important than it is now and young people continue to flock to it.

Dentistry

Gidday. If you've ever walked into a room and had everyone in it try to get out through a very small air vent, you probably know what it feels like to be a dentist. You have to be a fairly resilient sort of character because you have to spend all day seeing people who don't want to see you. Let's just take a typical dentistorial episode and give it the once over. You, the dentist, enter your surgery with considerable foreboding and seated in the waiting room is your first patient, Mr Jones, hiding behind a big stack of *Illustrated London News*, with only his feet sticking out. You put on your white backwards-coat, and you go out and tell Mr Jones that he can come in now. Then you prepare your little glass tray full of instruments and you go out and tell Mr Jones that he can come in now. You should have a record card for every patient so you go and get Mr Jones' card, you have a look at it and you tell him that he can come in now. Then you go over to your nurse/receptionist and inform her that she can tell Mr Jones that he can come in now. The patient will now look around the waiting room just in case there are some other Mr Joneses before him who've slipped down behind the heater and, having ascertained that he's the only major contender, he will eventually shuffle into your surgery and sit down.

You can try to make conversation with him if you like. My own personal advice is to leave him alone and just sing to yourself while you look at his X-rays and mutter about his upper left five and the watch on his dorsal cusps. When you peep into his throat you'll feel the tension in his nervous system and you'll notice the perspiration roaring out of his forehead and running down into his ears, so get your repair work done as rapidly as possible or he'll short everything and blow your surgery into a less desirable area.

Once you've laid your cement you will have to leave him there until it dries, with his mouth open and the little bilge pump on overdrive. If you hide around the corner during this period you'll notice that he does things like trying to line his feet up with the new carpark building, and inspecting your ceiling as if he's thinking of putting one in exactly the same at his place, or moving his head up and down so that the aeroplanes fly along in between the slats on the venetian blinds. The fellow's obviously a lunatic and you should get him out of your surgery as soon as possible. That's the main trouble with dentistry, you meet a very strange class of person. Actually, I recommend you stay away from dentistry altogether. See you in six months.

The Medical Profession

Gidday. I want to have a fairly detailed look at the medical profession so if the medical profession would just please take it's clothes off and cough ever so slightly, we'll get on with it. Unfortunately, not everyone can be a doctor. There simply isn't enough money to go around. So we'd better put you through the aptitudinatorial test just to see if you measure up.

Question 1: If a patient comes into your rooms complaining of a suspected sprain in the ear lobe sustained when his Rolls Royce hit his yacht, would you

(a) tell him to get out and stop wasting your time and take his malingering, complaining and patently transparent story to some other doctor with nothing better to do than sit round listening to the childish fabrications of obvious drunkards and the bone idle;

(b) tell him it's a psychosomatic secondary viral infection and continue practising your chip and run; or

(c) book him into a quiet little hospital, do tests on him for everything short of an ovarian cyst, invite him to dinner, clean his shoes, wash his car and explain to him that most of the fee is covered by the public health system?

The answer here is, of course, (c).

Question 2: If a patient comes to you with consumption and lungs full of coal dust, do you

(a) tell him to stop malingering and wasting your time and making excuses for his habitual drinking and wife beating;

(b) tell him it's a psychosomatic secondary viral infection and see if you can't get your putting a little better from another angle with the ball running against the grain of the carpet instead of with it; or

(c) whip him into a private hospital for a couple of weeks' complete rest, run a few tests on him, have him round for a feed and give him your car for the afternoon?

And the answer we're looking for here is (b). It used to be (a) but things have improved out of sight in recent years.

Question 3: If a woman comes to see you about some sort of problem in the ovipositer, do you

(a) tell her it's nothing;

(b) tell her it's nothing much;

(c) tell her it's nothing serious;

(d) tell her it happens;

(e) tell her it sometimes happens;

(f) tell her it happens from time to time;

(g) tell her to discuss it with her mother; or

(h) ask her if she's seen a doctor about it?

And, of course, the answer should be all of the above.

If you're up to it you might even like to become a specialist, but more about that some other time. I'm due at the golf course and someone else is on call so you'll have to excuse me. Please enjoy the music.

More Gauze

Gidday. It is with pride and not a little humility that I can announce that the Public Health System, which has been closed for renovations since August of last year, has now been completed and will be re-opened on Tuesday by the Minister for Money. It's new name is The Private Health System but otherwise everything is exactly the same unless you get sick. The two principal attractions of the new regime are that fees will rise and the medical profession will at last be spared the unsavoury and not very rewarding task of administering to the poor. Doctors will be put through a rigorous training programme to familiarise them with the demands of the new arrangements.

The training programme has been designed by experts and is extremely intensive, so if you miss something here you really will have great difficulty catching up. The course is necessarily fairly broad in its emphasis and you will need to grasp the general principles of medicine if you hope to go on to our specialist training later in the tax year.

Right, now I should point out that you will need first and foremost a licence to drive an articulated truck because, of course, you'll need to be able to shift your income about with you after work. You'll need a stethoscope, or something else to put in your ears so you don't have to hear those tiresome announcements about the Consumer Price Index and inflation and other evils caused by the disaffected, the unemployed and the disadvantaged.

You'll also need a map, of course, and if you go to the relevant planning authority you'll be able to get one which has got coloured sections on it so you can buy your hobby farm in an area that's earmarked for development. These areas go through the roof every couple of years and they hold their value very nicely even during a recession, which is quite important. I wouldn't bring it up normally of course but apparently there is a bit of a recession from time to time. They're caused by the unions, and if you're not careful property values can stagnate on you and, as I always say, if property's not moving where's the incentive to heal people?

Psychology

Gidday. I'd like to have just one or two words with you, through the chair, if I may, about becoming a psychologist. And it's important here to realise why society needs psychologists. What is the reason for psychology? In fact, what is psychology?

Well, of course, psychology is the business of getting hold of things that have happened for millions of years and giving them names. And very good names some of them are, too. For instance let's have a look at getting up in the morning. People have been getting up in the morning for a fair old while now, certainly since the war, and it's probably going to go on for some years to come. So psychologists give it a name; in this case the 'ante-nocturnal pre-micturitional departure of the scratcher' syndrome. Of course, Freud would go further and make certain uncalled-for suppositions about why you went to bed in the first place. He might even suggest manifestation of the 'post-hotel-going-back-to-your-place-for-a-bit of-the-old-loin-gratification' reflex. And Jung would just giggle and point at you, and if Reich came in you'd be well advised to confine yourself to rank and serial number.

Of course, the main call for psychologists comes from people who aren't very happy and who therefore exhibit the 'I'm not very happy' syndrome; and it's the psychologist's job to find out what is the cause of the unhappiness. This is where the psychologist displays 'the pig's back' syndrome and 'the falling-off-a-log' reflex.

The method whereby he finds out why people are not happy is that he asks them. The unhappy person then outlines the things that have engendered the onslaught of the anti-laughter factor and the psychologist then explains to the person why it is that he's not happy, calling everything by its correct psychological name and making another appointment so the person can come back in a couple of weeks and see what the psychologist was talking about the first time.

It's not a bad life actually, and it's particularly interesting if you have a tendency to the 'very large house full of consumer durables' syndrome reflex.

Accounting

Gidday. If you want to become part of the modern world I recommend you become an accountant more or less immediately. First of all, let's just see if you're aptitudinally suited to this lofty calling. I'd like you to be so good as to answer the following questions.

Can you count to three? (You may use a calculator during the final stages of your working, although it's probably better to lease one than to buy one, because the leasing of business machinery can be deductible at full rate, whereas purchase price, although deductible through charges against the current account and again advantageous through depreciation, is ultimately going to show up as an item of capital expenditure, and the opportunity cost of such utilisation of funds is obviously going to be the possible write-back to standard value of any cattle purchased before balance date and held subject to fertiliser provided by the vendor with monies other than those already earmarked for consideration as possible year one and year two input figures for a forestry development programme with milling at year one plus 23.)

Secondly, can you lean back in a chair, look out the window and demonstrate what's meant by the term 'a sharp intake of breath'? This is to be done whenever a non-accountant attempts to count to three so it's got to be mastered fairly early on. Of course, if you want to be a cost accountant or an auditor you'll also have to be able to put your hands together as if you're praying and tap your incisors with the nails on your two forefingers. But that's really fairly advanced and should probably be left till later.

Finally, and this is the real nub of the matter, can you draw a line down from the top of a piece of paper to somewhere near the bottom and can you count to three on both sides of the line? This is the very lifeblood of accountancy and if you can do that you're not only halfway there, you're halfway back as well.

Membership of the Parliament

Gidday. Today I'd like to avail you of information garnered by the Fred Dagg Careers Advisory Bureau concerning the whys and wherefores of being a Member of Parliament.

How you go about becoming elected is up to you. It's pretty much anything goes in this area and there are very few whys and no wherefores, and I understand there aren't as many whithers as there were either. It's what you do once you're in there that's important, and it'd be just as well to sit the bureau's aptitude test right at the outset just to see if you're suited to it. So pencils out, please.

If someone asks you a question in the House, do you

(a) accuse the other side of distorting the issue beyond all recognition and attempting to make cheap political capital out of something that should have been solved in the committee stages of the second reading of the recommendations of reports pursuant to amendments 129 and 130 of the Bill as laid down in Standing Orders and held by the Speaker in 1893 to be the right and proper duty of the

Member intituled the questioner;

    (b) answer the question; or

    (c) do anything in the world except (b)?

The correct response here is either (a) or (c). In fact that question's just been amended and (b) isn't there any more.

If a Member from the opposite benches rises to speak to the motion, do you

    (a) go to sleep;

    (b) shout "rubbish", "resign", "sit down" and "get out";

    (c) stand up with 19 points of order and then insinuate that the Honourable Member has been photographed at the Club Whoopee with his arm around a young woman of the opposite number; or

    (d) do (a) and (b) and (c)?

Fairly straightforward that one; (d) is the one we're after there.

If somebody got up one day and made a brilliantly intelligent and thoroughly worthwhile speech, would you

    (a) understand it;

    (b) understand it;

    (c) understand it; or

    (d) none of the above?

And here we're obviously looking for another (d).

So think about it, and if you've ever wanted to run away and join the circus, this could be the life for you.

Teaching

Gidday. I think it's time I had a word or two to say about the teaching profession. Now look! Some of you people at the back aren't paying attention, and if you think . . . who did that? Come on, who did that? I can wait, I've got all day. I can just wait here until that person owns up. We can all just sit here and wait. What's so funny? What's that . . . no . . . perhaps you'd . . . you, you, no, next to you . . . you, no next to you . . . you . . . yes, you, yes, perhaps you'd like to get up and tell us all the substance of your very amusing little remark. I think we'd all like to hear the joke, wouldn't we? We'd all like to have a laugh. Yes I think we could all do with a laugh. Nothing? Oh, I see, it's not funny any more. Well, isn't that interesting, the way jokes sometimes become a little less hilarious when we're asked to share them with our little friends.

Well, if I might be permitted to continue, I'd like to tell you about how to go about becoming a schoolteacher. Now, the first thing . . . stand up . . . stand up . . . you . . . no, behind you . . . no . . . behind you . . . yes, you, yes . . . stand up.

Well, Einstein, I take it that that magazine contains the answers to many of the problems we shall be confronting today. Who's that on the cover? I see, and who is Mr Travolta when he's at home? Oh, is he just? Well, I suggest that you put Mr Travolta away because you're not going to get anywhere in life by knowing a lot of nonsense about Mr Travolta. Are you listening to me? Are you listening to me at all? What did I say? What was the last thing I said? No, before that, smarty-pants! No, don't look out the window, don't look out the window when I'm talking to you. Look at me, Look at me, Look at me when I'm . . . I don't know why I bother. Who doesn't either? Come on, who just didn't either? Look, if people are going to "didn't either", I think I've got a reasonable right to know who they are. All right! I've had enough of this. I want you to write an essay on what you did in the holidays.

The Diplomatic Service

Gidday. I'd like to have a bit of a natter with you concerning the possibility that you could under certain circumstances consider the proposition that you might like to become a diplomat. Of course, I'm not suggesting that you're not perfectly happy doing what you're doing at the moment, and I certainly don't want to suggest that you're not very good at it. I'm sure you are; I'm sure you're excellent at it. In fact I'm told more or less constantly that without your steadying hand the whole place would fall apart. Neither do I mean to indicate that what you're doing is intrinsically inferior in any way to diplomacy. Very far from it. I know how valuable your work is and I hate to think what would happen if it wasn't done. The whole idea is absolutely unthinkable. And if anyone ever did anything to lessen the effectiveness of your work, I personally would release a decidedly cool statement, to be taken in the context of a joint communique which you and I would issue together, probably from a hotel foyer somewhere or with one of us at a lectern, confirming our mutual respect and reaffirming that our relationship can be expected to continue to produce ongoing dialogue of interest to all those with an interest in regional issues and in charting a viable course through the sensitive sargasso in which the Western power bloc finds itself at this difficult time in our history. Then we can hop out the back and I'll beat your face off.

If you're going to be a diplomat there's one thing you will have to face up to fairly early on in the piece; and that is that the human body can take only so much gin and tonic. You should probably work out your own capacity to the nearest bottle and have it engraved on a disc which you can hang around your neck. In cases of dire necessity, when you've driven your Elan into a swimming pool, medical authorities can administer the relevant dose to bring you back up to a fully functioning quota. Otherwise you can get into terrible trouble. I knew a bloke once who drank too much goat's milk at a diplomatic ball and discovered next morning that he'd annexed the back of Raetihi to part of Persia in exchange for 57 dozen pairs of sandals and a bathmat. So you'll have to watch yourself fairly carefully.

Of course, being a diplomat does involve a fairly comprehensive study of languages and you should probably have about half a dozen different languages up your sleeve. And you should have sufficient mastery of them that you can say absolutely nothing at all in any one of them. You should also study very closely the countries that you're working with, so that you can say absolutely nothing at all in the context of history. Familiarity with computer technology will enable you to transmit absolutely nothing at all at incredible speed directly on to someone else's hard disk and you should obviously have a reasonable facility in English so that you can say absolutely nothing at all several different ways at different press conferences and resist all attempts to trap you into saying anything other than absolutely nothing at all.

Becoming an Economist

Gidday. Sooner or later you should probably give a bit of consideration to becoming an economist. Of course, there are many thousands of economists about at the moment, although obviously as soon as we have an economy again they'll have to get off TV and radio and go back to work. This will cause an increase in demand and, to meet this, the supply will need to show an upturn sufficient that the marginal propensity to consume will be offset by the extent to which the diminishing returns can be kept in check by the savings and investment curve, with particular reference to the effect net of depreciation of a concomitant movement in the volume of overseas investment related to the internal devaluation factor and the disposable income of market leaders deriving income from dividends outside government stock.

Clearly, if the propensity for consumption does increase beyond a point where the marginal diminishing increase in production of durables can be expressed in terms of plus or minus the housing loans multiplier and the savings bank retentions, then we will see investors moving towards a liquidity preference, and savings will rise back above the original parabolic supposition. Keynesian theory and non-Keynesian theory, although of course not anti-Keynesian or pre-Keynesian theory, recognise this as being a problem soluble only by manipulation of the public purse to stimulate foreign investment or internal production of non-durables, to take up the slack in domestic spending net of sales tax. In other words, one plus one is equal to two, plus or minus the increased marginal propensity for tendencies.

Of course, this is all fairly self-evident and, if you can stay awake for more than three or four hours on the trot, I think you have the whole matter well in hand.

Television Drama

Gidday. I'd like to reveal to you one of the better guarded of the post-war vocational secrets, and that is how to write a domestic television drama. Before going any further I feel I should point out that, although there's a lot of public deprecation of the genre, this is largely an exercise in intellectual snobbery and in actual fact there's nothing wrong with it at all. It is a perfectly legitimate reflection of life as it is lived in the modern day and age and, although it is dramatised for maximum effect, it has more integrity than you could probably shake a stick at. It's all in the way you treat your subject matter. I'll just outline a simple plot which is not sensationalised and is true to life in every particular, just to show you that it can be done.

The show opens with the return home from university of a young man who's been away studying and who's come back because his father has unfortunately passed away during a break for station identification. When he arrives he gets a bit suspicious about the way people are carrying on and it dawns on him that his father might have been murdered by his uncle, a man named Claud. The uncle's actually not a bad bloke but he's always wanted the family business and in fact for some time he's been having the odd game of cachez le sausage with the young lad's mother. There are a couple of ghost scenes here where the lad talks to his father, but we can easily drop these if you think they're a bit unrealistic. I don't know that they work but the visual effects people won't let me touch them.

Anyway, being a red-blooded young fellow the student has a girlfriend and there are a few scenes here we'll have to drop, too, now I think about it; one in particular where he makes rather a lot of distasteful puns about her rural concerns and perhaps we could lose quite a lot of the audience if we're not careful. I didn't write this and now I come to read it properly I wonder whether it's suitable at all. It's Danish as a matter of fact. Perhaps I should have gone for something else. Anyway, I'll see if I can clean that bit up.

Anyway, the young student then does what so many young students do these days, he has a sort of nervous breakdown, or at least he pretends to and he fools everyone into thinking he's a few coupons short of a toaster. There's no mention of drugs in the story but obviously his mother in particular is very concerned about the sort of life he's been leading and what manner of person he's been hanging around with. And, of course, as so often happens in circumstances of this type, he has a series of very dramatic scenes with his girlfriend and he hurts her deeply. So distracted is she by his strange and possibly drug-crazed behaviour that she goes away and drowns herself in a river during another break for station identification. Then, of course, her family gets really quite litigious and her brother decides to nail him and there's a bit of a punch up at a rather suspect dinner party organised by the mother and this Claud rooster.

By now of course the young shaver's got his hands full because, aside from everything else, he's killed the girlfriend's father by stabbing him up the arras. We'll have to position about 97 cameras all over the studio because just about everyone gets finalised in one slightly ridiculous final scene.

The one big disadvantage of the story is that, although it's no more ludicrous than any of the other daytime TV plots, there aren't going to be enough characters left over at the end to get you into the second episode.

But give it a go anyway and if the public likes it I've got another little humdinger here about a very high-up black government official who snuffs his wife out because he thinks her handkerchief might have been carrying on with another bloke, and there's a beauty here about a crippled king and another little cracker about a transvestite lawyer and old man who bleeds when you prick him and goes to court over a meat deal. So if the TV industry runs out of unlikely plots for soapies there are acres of them in this book I've found.

Selling Insurance

Gidday. Many thousands of people have written to me asking how to become insurance agents and many have later written back thanking me for my advice and asking what insurance is. Let's not worry about what it is for a moment. That's not really the point with insurance. The insurance industry functions on two of our economic system's most hallowed precepts: greed, and fear of lack of greed. If everything that's insured was stolen or burnt down, there wouldn't be enough money ever printed in the history of the world to pay for it. But this doesn't matter because insurance companies are really selling something called 'peace of mind', which is not related to the real world except when you're paying for it. 'Peace of mind' is a marvellous thing to sell because you've still got it after you've sold it.

How do we achieve this miracle? I hear you cry.

Insurance is a financial concern so your ideal client is someone who doesn't know anything at all about finance and once you've cornered one of these balloons there are various ways to make your approach. If your victim has shiny trousers and is a mouth-breather you can often just worry him about how ill-prepared he is in the event of an attack on the family home by a 73-foot man-eating bat, and once you've got him on the run you can probably throw the book at him. Sell him a policy that protects him against the loss of anything he owns under any circumstances whatsoever except if he loses something. Sell him an all-risks policy on his house that provides him with the full and total value of the dwelling as assessed by you in the event of any loss or damage or impairment due to any cause other than those specified on pages 4, 5, 6, 7, 8, 9, 10, 11, 12, 15, 19, 33 and 48-79 of the attached schedule of authorised repudiations. Sell him a policy that protects him absolutely and provides his widow with a few draks if he's hit by a falling conifer while fishing at over a depth of about full fathom five.

You can charge about a dollar a year for some of these and you'll find that most people think it's one of the great bargains of the decade. Of course, if your prey is a little more sophisticated you might have to try a ruse or two. One of the more well-tested ruses is to engage someone in conversation about insurance, outline a very expensive policy and intimate that the monkey in question couldn't afford it because he's really just a common little nouveau with not too much under his hat and no taste and no lineage to speak of. What normally happens at this point is that the bloke will feel insulted and order a truck-load of the deluxe model. Either that or he'll laugh for a fair while and then plant you like a tree. Of course, if you could insure yourself against running across insurance salesmen, the world would be a superior venue altogether.

Real Estate

Gidday. Now the Fred Dagg Careers Advisory Bureau has already done enough to secure its place in the social history of this once great nation but I think this report is probably among its more lasting achievements. In essence it outlines how to go about the business of being a real estate agent (and as things stand at the moment, if you're not a real estate agent, then you're being a fool to yourself and a burden to others).

Like so many other jobs in this wonderful society of ours, the basic function of the real estate agent is to increase the price of something without actually producing anything and as a result it has a lot to do with communication, terminology and calling a spade a delightfully bucolic colonial winner facing north and offering a unique opportunity to the handyman.

If you're going to enter the real estate field you'll need to acquire a certain physical appearance which I won't bore you with here but, if you've got gold teeth and laugh-lines around your pockets, then you're through to the semis without dropping a set.

But the main thing to master, of course, is the vernacular, and basically this works as follows. There are three types of house: 'glorious commanding majestic split-level ultra-modern dream homes' that are built on cliff-faces, 'private bush-clad inglenooks' that are built down holes, and 'very affordable solid family houses in much sought-after streets' that are old gun-emplacements with awnings. A 'cottage' is a caravan with the wheels taken off. A 'panoramic', 'breathtaking', 'spectacular' or 'magnificent' view is an indication that the house has windows and, if the view is 'unique', there's probably only one window.

I have here the perfect advertisement for a house, so we'll go through it and I'll point out some of the more interesting features; so here we go, mind the step.

'Owner transferred reluctantly instructs us to sell' means the house is for sale.

'Genuine reason for selling' means the house is for sale. 'Rarely can we offer' means the house is for sale. 'Superbly presented delightful charmer' doesn't mean anything really but it's probably still for sale. 'Most attractive immaculate home of character in prime dress-circle position' means that the thing that's for sale is a house. 'Unusual design with interesting and intriguing solidly built stairs' means the stairs are in the wrong place. 'Huge spacious generous lounge commands this well-serviced executive residence' means the rest of the house is a rabbit warren with rooms like cupboards. 'Magnificent well-proportioned large convenient block with exquisite garden' means there's no view but one of the trees had a flower on it the day we were up there. 'Privacy, taste, charm, space, freedom, quiet, away from it all location in much sought-after cul-de-sac situation' means it's not only built down a hole, it's built at the very far end of the hole. 'A must for you artists, sculptors and potters' means that only an idiot would consider actually living in it. '2/3 bedrooms with possible in-law accommodation' means it's got two bedrooms and a tool shed. 'Great buy', 'ring early for this one', 'inspection a must', 'priced to sell', 'new listing', 'see this one now', 'all offers considered', 'good value', 'be quick', 'inspection by appointment', 'view today', 'this one can't last', 'sole agents', 'today's best buy' means the house is still for sale and if ever you see 'investment opportunity' in the newspaper, turn away very quickly and have a crack at the crossword.

Advertising

Gidday. I must say that we down at the bureau had a very enjoyable time researching this one. On the first day, we kicked off with a light lunch that lasted about five hours. Then we took the idea over to our creative department who recommended we get in touch with some of the people over in 'Concepts'. 'Concepts' went out and had not a bad lunch on it and came back with a story board which we tested in an open-ended, one-to-one market sample situation. Actually, we did this in Bangkok (we were going up there anyway for lunch so it wasn't too far out of our way). Next we went to Paris for a couple of days to throw a few ideas around and get some different coloured felt pens, and then on to Rio for lunch. On the way back I ran into a bloke who used to be AE with O & M before we both went across to Burnetts when Pattersons had burgled the MDA account from Hertz Walpole. He's now creative director with Silvergold Finklestein Gefilterfish and Baumbaum, and works out of New York. So we went over to his office for a short snort before lunch and he went over the whole concept with a fine tooth comb, right down to the media schedules and the market mixes. And ultimately he recommended that I conduct this lecture on the 'Clive James Show', the 'Oprah Winfrey Show' and 'Playschool' coupled with in-store promotion, pop-out full-colour, relief poster point-of-sale material and a radio and TV saturation campaign featuring Michael Jordan doing an old Beatles number with the critical message in the gaps between the choruses. It's a nice idea. I like it. I like it a lot and after lunch I'll decide what to do about it.

Making Investments

Gidday. I'd like to have a few words with you about the very vexed business of making investments. This is actually a leisure activity although some people get so carried away about it they hire office space and do it all week. This is a very dangerous attitude. Have your bit of fun by all means, but if you're thinking of taking it seriously I commend you to a little thing called 1929.

You will, of course, need a stockbroker. These are relatively easy to find running away from city buildings wearing stockings over their heads, agreeing that they don't officially know anything that isn't on the printout but remembering the names of people they went to school with. Then you start buying a few shares, just little ones to start with until you get the feel of it. And the thing to look for at all times is takeovers. If you own a few pieces of a small company that manages to get bought out by a big company and closed down and stripped of assets and all the staff gets fired, then that's very wonderful. Don't expect it to happen every time. (It does happen every time, but don't expect it every time or you'll lose the thrill of the chase.) Also be very careful about your jockey; sometimes a good prospect can be ridden badly or maybe the turf's had a bit much rain or something. And watch the supplementary number, too. And watch that the guy doesn't flip the coin the same way all the time, make him do it from different heights. And never trust the dealer, and remember second player plays low, and if you lose a few hundred thousand you mustn't be too surprised.

ECONOMY

*The crowning achievement of the national advisory
service, as the sun set on the difficult seventies and we witnessed
the bright new dawn of the brainless eighties, was the instructive
and detailed analysis pumped out on the economy and its
day-to-day management. There can be no more honourable
undertaking in all the estate of mankind. All stand please.*

Taxation Problems

Gidday. The question of taxation, which I recall having a bit of a ramble about the other day, is of great importance to the national economy, and before we go very much further it's probably not a bad idea if I just outline for you some of the more glaring shortcomings of the present system.

As you know, the government is very concerned about keeping inflation down. They don't know how to do it but I understand they're very concerned about it. And, of course, we're being asked to do various things in order to keep the gaskets from blowing again.

Normally, I wouldn't want to mention this at all but in the national interest I really do feel in all conscience that I should point out that the single most inflationary influence in this system at the moment is taxation. If you earn a dollar (and I'm not suggesting that you do) you pay income tax on it. Then you use it to buy something and the shopkeeper pays income tax on it and the person to whom it is paid by the shopkeeper then pays income tax on it. This process goes on until the dollar is so worn out it couldn't pull the skin off a rice pudding, much less defend itself against inflation.

Comprehensive research by the bureau's clinical division has determined that the average dollar in circulation at the moment is taxed 7325 times, and this means that the government nets something in the region of $3500 on every dollar there is. Clearly, this puts enormous pressure on the other dollars because, not only are they being taxed over 7000 times, they're being decimated at first base in order to defray the taxation bill on the previous dollar, and, with the government's own policies causing inflation of 3500 per cent to start with, I think the rest of us aren't doing a bad job to keep the overall figure down to around double what the government promised it would be by last Xmas at the very latest. Obviously there's something wrong here. There has to be some method whereby the government can be forced to act responsibly and stop holding itself to ransom. The only other possibility is that somebody out there believes that inflation is a good, dependable, non labour-intensive growth industry that should be maintained at all costs. I'll have a closer look at this. It's a possibility we can't entirely discount. At least I don't think we can. Perhaps if we put it in the children's name we can discount part of it. I'll have a look.

Interest Rates

Gidday. I'd like to think I've talked enough about interest rates by now but, on the other hand, it is perhaps time I actually said something about them because as you can see they've packed their gear up and they're obviously going somewhere whether we like it or not. And I would make the point that when I said they wouldn't go up I was really just preparing the ground for my real opinion, which was that they'd go down. And by 'down' I meant not as far up as a lot of people were saying at the time. 'Down' wasn't exactly the right word to describe this projection. I realise that now and, if I had my time again, I'd say that I fully expected interest rates to go down but with another word in there instead of 'down'.

'Up' probably. 'Up' is the obvious one. I can't think why I didn't think of it at the time. 'Up' is a much more likely place for them to have gone, as witness their subsequent rise, which has, of course, taken place in that direction. However, as to present circumstances, there's been a good deal of pressure on interest rates and this came to a head the other day with the Reserve Bank Bond Tender (an old and very trusted friend of many of us here today) struggling in the face of a bull element in the private market.

The inevitable increase in related percentages will not have a marked effect on the other indices. There will be adjustments made but they'll be in the nature of fine tuning. We have to be realistic about these things. We've done everything we can to keep them down by pretending they wouldn't go up but in the final analysis it's the market itself that determines the movement of the variables and, if I might be permitted one final comment, I would just say that at this stage we've got every hope that they'll come down even further some time next year.

Understanding the Budget

Gidday. A great many people are confused by certain aspects of the economic miracle from which we are all currently suffering. For example, the central planning document is the national Budget, a complex document, and the public often fails to grasp its significance. This may be due in part to the fact that press analysis of budgetry policy is conducted by five-year olds or by people associated with the formation of the policy but, for heaven's sake, I do wish people would stop complaining. I think it's time you woke up to yourselves. There's no point in having the young fellow standing around sticking his finger in and out of the hole in the dyke if all you people are going to do is wander about the place being grumpy.

Running the country is just like running a household and I don't know whether you've ever had your household run by Her Majesty's Opposition but after about 18 months the whole place lifts completely off the ground and, unless you got down on a travel grant before they introduced hydraulic round-the clock inflation, you'll find yourself spending less and less time with your family.

And, as you know, this is precisely the position we inherited. We've been able to patch up bits of it since we got in certainly, but Rome wasn't built in the whole of the post-war period with two very slight gaps and there are elements of the way things are going at the moment that would disturb anyone. But I do wish people wouldn't get so disturbed about them.

Work is the thing that'll pull this country out of the already superb position it's in now to an even better position. People have simply got to realise that only by working extremely hard and not stopping all the time to ask for more money or part of a condition can we improve the state of this country. Well, some of the states of this country. Some of the other states I'm afraid we'll have to mark as absent.

But we can't be expected to look after everything, anyway. You can't look after everyone. You've got to have priorities. We've got a list somewhere of the people we've been looking after. I haven't actually got it myself at the moment. The Finance Minister's got it. He's taking treatment for it but, as far as I know, he's still got it and, if your name doesn't appear on it, I must ask you to stop looking out the window and just get on with your work, or whatever it is you people do with your time.

Lateral Banking

Gidday. Advancements in thought can often be of great and lasting value to society as a whole. I'd like to have a word or two with you about what I think is now widely recognised as the single most important philosophical development of the modern age. I'm talking here, of course, of the ideas embodied in my seminal work 'Lateral Banking', which I published some years ago now under the nom de pseud Edward de Daggo.

As you may subsequently have observed, I've found an industrial application for my work in more recent times and I'd like to explain roughly how this works (or as I prefer to say "I'd like to explain its 'workness'").

Obviously one of the most serious problems confronting the industrial nations at the moment is industrial relations and it's not really possible to put everyone involved in industry through some sort of Relational Interface Therapy, so quite clearly a totally new overall approach is required. The problems involved in industrial relations differ, of course, with time and place, and one of the difficulties has always been that the solutions have been equally diverse and the solution in one case might be inapplicable in another.

Although it might not be immediately apparent, there is a consistent quality in all the solutions and that quality can be defined by the fact that, to a given degree, those problems have been solved. They have acquired what I call "solvedness". And it can be said that, rather than having many solutions, we have "solvedness" which is simply applied in many different ways.

Equally, of course, we have "problemness" which manifests itself in various forms and places.

And in order to counter the now consistent and identifiable "problemness" with the easily recognisable "solvedness" (and I don't want to go into a needless amount of detail here, it'll only confuse you and this has probably cost you "smallfortuneness" already so I'll give you this in a nutshell) we need to provide a balance between "problemness" and "solvedness" and unfortunately I don't really think at the moment I've got time to run through the concept of "balanceness".

Someone will now pass among you with millinery and I'll get back to you about this as soon as you come up with a deposit.

The Hidden Unemployed

Gidday. Even during a rigorous and, as in the current case, blisteringly exciting election campaign, the government must ensure that the economy is working. And I don't know whether or not you noticed this in the run up to the cliffhanger but some new unemployment figures were released last week and, if you thought unemployment was high beforehand, you might like to just grab your hat and go for a little stroll while the rest of us go through this for spelling mistakes.

The reason that the new figures are a bit more lofty than the style to which we've become accustomed is that someone has included some of the unemployed in the calculations.

The unemployed who have been included this time are called 'the hidden unemployed', which means they're the same as the rest of the unemployed in that they're unemployed but they've been hidden from us by not having been mentioned in unemployment figures. And if you're not going to mention the unemployed in unemployment figures, it's highly unlikely that they're going to show up anywhere else unless they go overseas and are somehow recorded as invisible exports.

But the main thing about them is that there are 500,000 of them and, if they're added to the other group of un-hidden unemployed, we're looking at about 900,000 although, of course, you can't see the whole group because 500,000 of them are hidden behind things.

But let's make no mistake about the country. The country is lucky. I don't know whether you've ever seen it from the air but the higher you get the luckier it looks (and this applies on the ground as well, of course).

I must admit I was very surprised about the 500,000 hidden unemployed. It hadn't occurred to me that some people are sufficiently disheartened to just give up and not even register as unemployed. This is a big surprise to me. I had no idea about this and none of the other people around here have had any idea for a long time, which might be part of the problem, although I do wish someone had hidden it better.

LEISURE

*Equally valuable, of course, has been the bureau's work
in the area of leisure and recreation. Being a New Zealander,
Mr Dagg has been in an excellent position to engage in
many years of comprehensive immersion in almost
every known form of leisure pursuit.*

Photography

Gidday. I want to talk to you about a very serious leisure activity, one that already has adherents by the oodle and as a time-consumer it's regarded very highly by tall people. I'm referring here, of course, to photography. Photography, from the Latin word camera.

For this activity you'll need either quite a lot of very expensive gear with fittings, adaptors, tripods and light meters, or some cheap gear and a fairly fertile imagination. You've probably all seen those superb photos of humming birds being born in *Life* magazine and the first thing to do is to forget all about those because they're not photos at all. They're all just made up to look like photos. As a matter of fact, I knew the bloke who used to make them up and many's the time we've had a good laugh about the way the world fell for it. He used to get an old drawing and colour it in with a felt pen until it looked real and then he'd photograph it from the air through a gauze bandage. Then he'd claim to have taken the original up the Amazon with a Corthon Pentbox 28.329 double-macro zoom-aperture flange-gasket and no one ever found him out. But anyway they aren't photos, those things. Photos are the things you've got at home in black-paged books with your sister's boyfriend cut off at the chin and that good one of Uncle Arnold hiding behind the milkman's horse. Anyone can take these and, although we can't cover the whole field here, we can look at one example.

Let's say you want to take a photograph of a friend. In fact, let's go further than that and say you've got a friend. You place your friend in position, some easy position in case it takes a while to get the light right and your friend gets tired of standing on one hand with a fruit bowl on his nose while you get the camera ready.

If it's daytime you set the pointer to the correct setting and if it's night-time the advice of the professionals is to drop off into some snorage until it's daytime because you can't take proper photos at night. For that you need a flashlight and it's a well-known fact that a flash only works when you turn it around to see why it didn't work. You set the film speed and the aperture and the shutter speed at the correct settings and you tell your friend you'll be ready in half a second.

Then you whack your nose down on to the little hole and look through the framing set-up and work out how if your friend helps you here you might be able to take the best photo in the history of the English-speaking snapshot with the shadow of a cathedral across his cheek and the rubber factory coming out his ear. So you move him around till he's in the right place, which he never is because he can't tell left from right and he moves backwards all the time and keeps walking forward out of focus to hear what you're saying because you're talking into the rewind button. Eventually, he ruins the whole thing and you end up taking a shot of a seagull hovering about 150 kilometres off the coast. It won't be visible in the shot and you know it won't, but you went out to take a photo and no idiot friend is going to spoil a good relaxing leisure day.

Writing a Novel

Gidday. In the following little bagatelle I'd like to have a few words with you about becoming a novelist. I address myself to this subject in response to many zillions of letters I've received from persons claiming to be latent or potential novelists. Here's a sample, just to give you an idea of the type of thing we're knee-deep in down at the bureau.

"Dear Fred. I think I have a novel in me. I think perhaps we all do. Signed, Budding Novelist." Here's another one: "I've always wanted to write a really good novel. At the moment everything I do is just a little bit boring. I hope this comes right with time. I'm writing this for a friend. Signed, P. White." And thanks very much Perce and, of course, there are countless others along similar lines.

Clearly there are many novelists out there fermenting and just waiting for the muse to spirit them into print. So I think this is probably a suitable moment to whistle through some of the more fundamental do's and don'ts of the novel-writing caper in general.

The first thing to decide is what sort of novelist you'd like to be: a tall novelist, a short novelist or a novelist of medium stature, a modern novelist, a neo-classicist or a pastoral stream-of-consciousness gothic feminist. And once you've made this decision you're halfway there, really.

Next, of course, you've got to sit down and pound out your actual novel, beginning each new sentence with a capital and numbering the pages very carefully. There's nothing more frustrating to the reader than getting right through a novel and then discovering that it was read in completely the wrong order.

You'll need a main character (a protagonist will probably do if you don't mind cutting a few corners) and you'll need a plot of some sort. This is really just a device to give you something to write about while your main character's in the toilet or changing hats or something. And once you've got your plot worked out you'll have to develop some manner of style.

Now when it comes to style in the novel, it is instructive to browse through history and see what's available. First of all there's the first person, which is 'I', or in this case 'you', which is the second person, and 'he', 'she' or 'it', which are the third person, except 'it', of course, which isn't a person at all, and whatever you're having yourself.

The novel was begun in a hotel called The Mists, which is just outside Antiquity. It was begun by several people and Richardson was one of them. Samuel Richardson his name was (he's probably dead now, he was a very old man when I knew him) and he wrote a thing called *Pamela*, which established two great strains which run through all subsequent history of the novel: the use of the narrator and boredom. The story was fairly simple and it concerned promiscuity, attempted rape, submission and other burning issues of the day. It was basically a diary and the style was a good example of what scholars refer to as 'awful'.

You could, of course, do worse then emulate the style of Dickens, who wrote mainly for periodicals and, as a result, has a fair number of his characters down a snake pit on a rope which is being burnt with a fire by a man-eating tiger at the end of each week's little capsule. This gives his novels more climaxes per chapter than most novelists could handle, and it embodies Dickens' claim to be 19th century literature's equivalent of 'Neighbours'.

Then you've got your Tolstoy, of course, who came from a small village in England called 'Russia'. He experimented with the novel to see how thick it could get. And he discovered that with proper attention it could get very thick indeed. And he sold the film rights and died in his own personal railway station.

D.H. Lawrence should not be imitated without medical supervision as he was captain of the Nottingham raincoat brigade, and in later life had a brush with an outfit called the Bloomsbury Set who make Liberace look like a football team.

James Joyce is really the prince of style and, if you're looking for a style for yourself or perhaps a nice little style for a friend of the family, I recommend that you look very closely at James Joyce and Walt Disney.

By now your novel should be coming along quite nicely and in the interests of artistic integrity, which is basically a marketing concept, it's probably time to address yourself to the difficult task of injecting local flavour into it because, of course, the greatest possible achievement for the scrivener is to come up with The Great New Zealand Novel.

In this pursuit there are several cardinal rules. Firstly, if you've got any interesting characters in mind, drop them immediately or you'll ruin everything. If there's one thing that The Great New Zealand Novel should not have under any circumstances whatsoever, it's an interesting character. By all means have a main character, but ideally he should be a character of unexampled tedium. In fact, he should never actually do anything. Things can happen to him by all means, but he's a victim at all times and never an initiator of an action. And the things that happen to him should, so far as is possible, be boring.

If you find that for some reason or other you do have an interesting character, have him shot about halfway down page one by a boring character. Make it obvious that the boring character didn't actually decide to shoot the interesting character, he was forced to do it by the crushing heartlessness of the post-war fusion of urban and rural society, in which process the doctrine of free will is emasculated by the power of capital and the stark hostility of the land itself (I'm sorry, the stark hostility of the *very* land itself). Of course, the main character should be a testament to the alienation of mankind from the pantheistic subtleties inherent in his world. And he should demonstrate with frightening clarity the tragedy of self-deception and man's inhumanity to woman.

Have your novel published by some university in the Chathams in a run of a couple of dozen and if nobody reads it you'll be up there with the giants.

Poetry

Gidday. Now, as a result of the more or less runaway success of the bureau's recent analysis of the English novel and how to write one, I'd like to have a few words with you today about another aspect of the literary field, and I'm referring here, of course, to the very wonderful world of poetry.

You've probably all heard of poetry but for those of you who've actually studied it, we'd better start at the beginning. A poem, very briefly, is a short novel you can foxtrot to.

Poems have a regular beat, not counting anything by Gerard Manley Hopkins, the inventor of calypso, and these beats are called iambs, or feet, from the French jambe, or leg, and they're measured on a little indicator called a pentameter, which records the metric rhythm of a poem and it lights up and emits a loud buzzing noise if there's a mistake or an Alexandrine or something, although they sometimes go off if someone in the next room turns on a hairdryer, so they're not infallible. This is the reason university English departments cut themselves off from the outside world, because if a pentameter throws a valve or the bulb goes or something, they've got to write away to the 17th century to get the parts manual.

The only other things about poetry are that it rhymes, except on certain occasions when it doesn't, and that all poems are about flowers. This is really the cardinal rule. Even poems that aren't about flowers are about flowers. Even if a poem is about a battle it'll have all the soldiers falling over like hollyhocks and nurturing the soil and throwing away their pistils, and if they get through it they all go into town and pollinate themselves to a standstill.

This is called symbolism and I want to point out right at the outset, it is not for the faint-hearted. I spent several years trying to direct my attention to poetic symbolism and believe you me it's not all beer and skittles. I caught rather a lot of viruses and my grandmother passed away every second Thursday for nearly four years, so if you think this is going to be a pushover my advice to you is get out now. Just move quietly to the back of the room and make your way out into the exercise yard. There's no shame in being a bit scared of it. It's better to be honest now when you've got the opportunity to jump off, than to pretend it doesn't worry you and then get yourself into trouble later. It's fair enough not to want to be part of this. I feel pretty bad about the whole thing myself. You didn't know when you first put your name down that we'd ever get into this sort of area. There's no compunction to stay at all. I feel you should know that. You're quite free to go.

Right, now for those of you who are left I've got just one further warning. It's a warning I think you have a right to hear and it's impossible for me to over-emphasise the gravity of what I'm about to say. I'll tell you this just once, and when you hear it I'd like you each to think very carefully before making a decision.

In the discussion of symbolism in English poetry, we'll be looking at a poem by William Wordsworth.

Right, now I see that some of you are beginning to see sense at last. You people who are staying, if necessary an oxygen mask will fall from the compartment above you. Please put it on. You'll find a life raft under the seat in front of you.

William Wordsworth. Wordsworth is often referred to as a lake poet, although why this is no one knows. It has been suggested that perhaps he looked a bit like a lake but this seems unconvincing. I think it's probably a misprint and what they really meant to say was that Wordsworth was a late poet. This certainly sounds more reasonable to me as we do know that Wordsworth paid the supreme sacrifice during the prickly-heat epidemic that motored through Grassmere in about 1850.

He was a curious fellow and he had very few friends: his sister Dorothy, a bloke called Samuel Taylor, and the poet Coleridge. Samuel Taylor did the lawns and fixed windows and things while Dorothy, Coleridge and Wordsworth sat around writing poetry and watching old movies.

The poem we're going to look at was originally intended for publication in *Lyrical Ballads*, and then again in *The Prelude*, but the manuscript went missing and turned up only recently in a trunk-full of old cricket bats in the lost property office at the Alfoxden Railway Station. It contains all Wordsworth's later English patriotism and is loaded with classical references echoing Hesiod and Virgil. You'll also notice the pantheism of the true nature poet creeping about within the narrative. I won't tell you any more. I'd like you to just read the poem for yourselves and appreciate for yourself the beauty of it, prior to scholarly analysis.

"There was a mathematician named Hall
Who had a hexagonal ball
The cube of its weight times its height plus eight
Is his phone number
Give him a call."

Now let's analyse the poem piece by piece and see what it means.

"There was a mathematician named Hall." This is fairly straightforward. The reference is to Sir Albert Hall, who was in Germany during 1798 when Wordsworth, Dorothy, Coleridge and Samuel Taylor went there to cover the European Swimming Champs for the *Spectator*. So "There was a mathematician named Hall."

Now: "Who had a hexagonal ball."

Here we have to go to some trouble to avoid jumping to an erroneous conclusion. As laid down by the great authority on symbolism, Ephraim, and more particularly by his son Ephraim (Symbolist) Junior, a ball in this context has its meaning in the ballistic sense and represents the Teutonic military obsession as exemplified by Hall, who was working for the Westphalian Cavalry trying to develop the tank for use in the upcoming rumble with Napoleon. And at this stage it was thought that a hexagonal cannonball was the ideal shape.

"The cube of its weight times its height plus eight
Is his phone number
Give him a call."

This is quite complicated. The telephone reference is a bit confusing because the phone wasn't in general use in 1798, although Samuel Taylor had actually invented the telephone as early as 1789. The only major mistake he'd made was that he'd invented only the first telephone and it was left to the American, Bell, to come up with the second telephone before the whole business could really get off the ground. The implication here is that once telephones had been properly developed, they'd fit a phone on to the cannon, Samuel Taylor would dial Napoleon's number and when the little master picked the receiver up he'd get hit in the ear with one of Hall's six-sided projectiles. And Wordsworth thought he'd worked out a formula for getting through to Paris without ringing the operator. When this information got back to the War Office, a lot of people thought Wordsworth had mislaid a marble, which was perfectly natural and this is why he was called a nature poet.

I hope you've absorbed all this because I won't be talking about poetry again. I got as far as Keats once and was obliged to send up flares and blow whistles until an airlift could be mounted.

Watching Old Movies

Gidday. I'd like to address your attention to the watching of old movies and in this context it's difficult to overestimate the value of the word 'old'. What the term 'movies' means here is difficult to say.

Of course, the major pitfall in this otherwise innocuous and soporific pastime is that, unless you watch yourself very carefully, you can become a movie buff and, if you think you recognised Lon Chaney's half-sister's ex-husband in the Cossack Army in the RKO remake of Scott Fitzgerald's *The Hootnanny at Dead Man's Gulch*, it's probably a good idea to go and have a few tumblers of the Bristol Cream or pretty soon you'll be spotting Greta Garbo's uncle and various Barrymores and Lunts and Gabors and things and it's only a short hop from there to the padded single bedroom.

Of course, you'll have to know a few key facts to help you stay above the waterline in the pulse-quickening banter about old films and I've taken the liberty of preparing a brief list for you so you'll be familiar with the basic rules.

The greatest actor in the history of the world was Humphrey Bogart. Alfred Hitchcock appears in his own films. Samuel Goldwyn said funny things a little bit like a four-year-old. Virginia Rapp. Marilyn Monroe was misunderstood and sensitive and loved Sibelius and was a brilliant actress. Dorothy Parker once said just about everything. Doris Day's real name was Adolf Schicklgruber. Bogart never said "play it again, Sam", although Dorothy Parker probably did. Citizen Kane is a kind of American Winebox Inquiry.

And that's about all you'll need to know if you want a bit of a dally in the realms of buffdom, although personally I suggest you just watch the films over your newspaper and treat them as one of life's little sideshows.

Chess

Gidday. I'd like to have a few words with you today about chess, a game which sometimes leaps into the news from nowhere due to the grapple which goes on from time to time for the world title.

Chess is, of course, an extremely intellectual game and indeed I've heard it referred to as a war game. Still, I've heard the health system referred to as enlightened so obviously the use of language has become fairly liberal, if that's not a contradiction in terms.

Chess is a very old game and it has a fair complement of well-established moves, gambits and patterns and if you're going to have a bash at it you'll need to familiarise yourself with some of these. First of all, let's have a look at some of the moves made by Messrs Karpov and Korchnoi during the great tussle of '81 and see if we can pick up a few pointers.

Karpov was apparently something of a traditionalist and was extensively schooled in the conventional parry and thrust, while Korchnoi was considered something of a daredevil and was likely to throw his pawns out the window and break into a Highland Fling when his opponent was expecting a Sicilian defence with the Hackaknackaroff variation.

Actually, Korchnoi had Karpov in all sorts of trouble in three or four games on the trot with a combination of imaginative knight placement and a series of quick-fire jabs to the face and body, but somehow he didn't press home his advantage. That's what you do with an advantage in chess, you press it home, although the idea of even getting an advantage against the likes of Karpov is enough to take the breath away and drain the blood completely from the face.

The reason that Korchnoi didn't press his advantage home in those games transpired to have been the fact that his owl died. He went into a period of deep gloom and spent a good deal of time resting in a brown study somewhere and in this brooding state he became unable to press home his advantage.

This is called Korchnoi's Complaint and, of course, Karpov was able to force draws in those contests, and the battle continued later with Korchnoi as fit as a buck rat and raring to go again. Korchnoi celebrated his return to form with a devastating game where he ran Karpov all over the place with a stunning attack down the left wing, featuring wide-ranging power from the Queen and Bishop coupled with insurmountable strength in the Rook-line and high lobs into the sun. Karpov put up a series of diversionary pawn attacks and tried to change the subject but Korchnoi wasn't taken in and he pressed home his advantage from all directions. After that it was just a matter of time.

Actually the whole business of playing chess is really just a matter of time and if you've got a couple of weeks up your sleeve I recommend you give it a lash.

Sewing

Gidday. As anyone who's ever drawn a few stitches together will tell you, sewing is a major usurper of time and, in terms of energy, an afternoon of pleating buttonhole darts is about equivalent to running a marathon with a cast iron stove strapped to each leg.

Let's just take a simple sewing exercise and see how the process operates. Let's say you want to do something fairly basic and everyday, like converting an old pair of jeans into a batik wall-hanging that doubles as a zip-up lampshade with pockets.

First of all, you'll need a sewing-machine, so you locate that and park it somewhere good and central. Then you have a go at fixing whatever it was that broke last time and caused you to put it away when you were trying to make a shirt out of the curtains.

Once you've got the little light going, you can lay your material out, and start cutting it out into shapes that you think might be roughly suitable. Within a matter of moments you'll have most of the room draped in a solid ocean of fabric, you'll have lost the scissors somewhere back at base camp three, and you'll have to set out on a separate expedition to find the sewing machine. Everyone else in the house will have suddenly remembered they've got important things to do on the other side of the moon, and when you lift the material up you'll notice that you've cut enough carpet out of the floor to make a series of matching winter overcoats for most of the people you've met since you left primary school.

Now you can get some of the hunks you've cut out and start trying to sew them together. You've got to be very careful at this stage, particularly with your foot. Unless you know how to work the accelerator properly, the machine will go into overdrive and sew a big line of blanket-stitch through everything that's not bolted to the floor. This doesn't last long though, because in no time at all you'll break the needle and fill the insides of the sewing machine with about a hundred thousand kilometres of intricately knotted cotton.

At about this stage you should give the whole thing away and leave in disgust, pulling the sewing machine over and dragging the whole room with you, since by now you'll have sewn the jeans to the couch and the tail of your shirt and the only advantage is that it'll expose the floor again and reveal a zillion small pieces of cotton that you can spend the rest of the day cleaning up.

If you weren't present at the sacking of Carthage I recommend you have a crack at sewing. It'll give you an idea of what the place must have looked like afterwards.

Card Tricks

Gidday. The ancient art of card trickery has taken a dive in the last 50 or 60 years due mainly to the invention and subsequent development of the motor car. This enabled whole groups to move at high speed away from people who were doing card tricks and, of course, the Wright Brothers, Wilbur and Mr Ed increased this speed and what with space travel the humble card trick has taken a clobbering all round. This is a shame, as the card trick is a well established time-waster and is good for at least an afternoon, and if it's raining it can give your whole weekend a bit of a surprise.

Card tricks were started back in what we historians call the olden days, by the patron saint of cards and off-course substitutes, St Leger de Main. He was a petty officer on a minesweeper during the Children's Crusade and, as you can imagine, the jolly jack tars had a bit of time on their hands. They played a fair amount of deck quoits and I understand some of them had masked balls, but after a few years they'd whittled it down to running on the spot and I Spy. One day St Leger and a mate of his were splicing the main mizzen fore stays'l cleat halyard and St Leger thought of the card trick. Some authorities don't agree entirely with this view of the derivation and have tried to minimise the role of St Leger in the conception. However, for the most part they are rather silly people and for my money the story has about it the tell-tale ring of truth.

Nowadays, of course, the card trick is used as a light amusement, principally by people who've just been thrashed at canasta and are prepared to go to any lengths to re-establish themselves as sentient human beings, even if it means finding the four of spades up the host's nose.

I'll demonstrate a couple of basic card tricks for you just to give you an idea of the advanced standard that's been reached since those early days.

Pick a card, any card. Have a look at it. Don't tell me what it is, just memorise it; you might like to whisper it to your loved ones. There it goes, back into the pack again. I'll just shuffle them all up so we don't know where it's gone. Now I'll cut the pack, there's nothing up my sleeves and the cards are all mixed up. Now I'll just reach over here behind this rabbit and underneath this glass of water and . . . Is this the card you chose? Of course it is. And have you ever met me? Have we ever seen each other before? No we haven't. Truly a piece of magic.

Here's another one. I'll just pull this card out of the middle of the pack. I can't see it, I don't know what it is. Unless I'm very much mistaken it's the queen of hearts. Yes, quite right. A lucky guess? Perhaps. Who knows? How do I do it? Ah no, I can't tell you that. It's magic. Another one? Sure, I've got thousands of them.

Try it for yourself and watch the hours and your family and friends slipping relentlessly away.

A Nice Drive

Gidday. What you'll need here is a car, preferably one with a few major mechanical defects, windows that don't open properly without a hammer and ideally, of course, the car should be just a tiny bit too small for the number of people you've got to put in it.

For the sake of getting to the main business of the drive itself I'll ignore the many potentially charming aspects of the planning stages, the preparation of food and clothing for the journey and a fair amount of reasonably heated discussion as to exactly where you're going to go.

Around about five hours after you planned to return, you should be leaving. The day should be overcast, cloud down to about 45 centimetres, visibility zero and falling. The temperature should be about 1000°Celsius on the Richter scale and the atmosphere would probably weigh in at around 95% water. You should have three in the front seat, or, if the car seats three in the front seat, you should have four in the front seat and in the back there should be a landscape of fairly small faces with perhaps a smattering of aunties, grandparents or some other mentally unhinged person with a bit of a death-wish.

The boot should be burgeoning with beetroot sandwiches and spare jerseys and there should be tea in thermoses and at least an oodle of cold sausages and bacon and egg pie, so if the drive gets a little tedious you could conceivably have a crack at the north face of the Eiger.

You are now prepared and, as you leave home wondering about whether you turned the stove off and hoping the cat doesn't get accidental behind the fridge, you begin to feel free and hopeful. You look out the window and everyone says "Isn't this fun" and "Shouldn't we do it more often". My advice to you is to enjoy this bit of the trip, savour it and let it linger on the palate. It's the last bit of enjoyment you'll have for a fair while.

When you're out in the unknown and the heat's appalling and you're up a side road that someone said was quicker but you can tell it isn't going to be, you should find your left back tyre's doing pancake impressions and it's a good thing you've got to pull over anyway because the temperature light's on, the oil light's flickering, the petrol-gauge only works downhill and if the smell's anything to go by, part of the fuselage is on fire.

This is the highlight of the outing in several respects. You've got to get the food out to get to the spare and you can have a go at the prandials while you work out why the spare's only got one metric puff of air in it and who you lent the jack to. By now the weather's getting its eye in and the sandwiches have melted, the kids have collapsed and the top's blown off the radiator.

When someone eventually comes to the aid of the party and you limp home on one cylinder, you may not feel you've had the greatest time of your life. You might not even want to see anyone else ever again. But there's no denying you've given Sunday a run for its money.

The Car

Gidday. A lovely little activity this one, just right for a young couple with a small family, trying to break into serious time-wasting but with an eye to the familial budget. Or for an older person perhaps, past doing wind sprints and not up to Wagner without a cuspidor, this is a well-established 100 per cent bona fide classic. I refer, of course, to the maintenance of a motorised conveyance.

Since the dawn of mankind, which has been pinpointed by carbon-dating at about 1921, the motor car has proved to be faulty, and the human being, in his ineffable desire for perfection and his fairly effable desire not to use buses and trains, has attempted to repair such disorders as arise by frightening them from underneath or cracking them with a spanner from above.

If you are going to devote yourself to car repairs, you'll need the following things: a car – any car, even one that's in what is sometimes risibly referred to as 'perfect working order', because as anyone with half a brain and a set of sockets will tell you, there's no such thing. Ideally, though, the car should be blighted by at least one major disorder like shot rings or a couple of thousand volts in the door handle.

You'll need overalls, or something so covered in grease you can't tell it isn't overalls. You'll need a spanner, a roll of tape, and a box to put all the things in that you've unscrewed and can't remember where you unscrewed them from, or why. You'll need a screwdriver, or else there'd be no point in having the box, and finally you'll need a jack. This is so the car can be raised to a sufficient height that you can sleep under it.

Let's take a simple everyday mechanical problem, and follow it through to get the idea of how these things are done by the experts. Let's say there's a knock in the engine and the indicators go on when you activate the cigarette lighter, the heater, the horn, or open the glove box on the driver's side.

The first thing to do is kick the tyres. Always kick the tyres before you do anything else. Just walk up to them, individually, look at each one briefly, and boot it. This is like hanging up a 'Work in Progress' sign and it serves fair notice to everyone within about a 16-kilometre radius that you'll be occupied until sundown. Next, you walk round to the front or 'bow' section of the offending vehicle and you whack the bonnet up and have a broad general kind of look at the donkey. Most of the trouble has its origins up in the nose-cone and it's as well to start here and eliminate things as you work your way back down the ground to the southern end, finishing in front of the sightscreen. Undo some nuts from somewhere and take one spark plug and the distributor cap and put them all in a little heap on top of the air-cleaner. Open the driver's door and go and have a cup of tea. The ground work is now done. All the traditional rituals have been observed.

In the afternoon, get yourself comfortable under the car and invite someone else to assist you. Sit your assistant in the pilot's chair and get him to push the brake, accelerator, clutch, brake, clutch, brake, accelerator and indicators while you tap the sump with the spanner. This incessant tapping should have you both in the arms of Morpheus fairly smartly and the only remaining custom is to state with some certainty when asked how the car's coming along, that you've broken the back of it and should have it running better by Xmas. Don't specify which Xmas, just use the word quickly and pack up your tools.

Plumbing

Gidday. Now, of course, it costs a great number of ducats to get an actual professional plumber around to do your plumbing, so amateur plumbing has been thrust on the bulk of the populace and the sooner you come to grips with it the better. Obviously the only people making enough money to get professional help in are plumbers, so the people who really need to develop a reasonably impressive array of plumbing skills are those among us who are non-plumbers and I might say that, in non-plumbing circles, I am accorded the status of grand master.

Let's just take a simple everyday run of the mill plumbing problem and work our way through it until we've solved it, and I'm using the word "solved" here for the metre.

Let's say you have a dripping tap. Let's say it's dripping in the same way that, say, Niagara drips. The first thing to do is to turn the water off outside at the mains. For this you'll need a machete, about four day's rations and a good map. Next, you should unscrew the dripping tap. You'll find it's on fairly tightly and you'll have to belt it a few times with a big hammer. This'll strip the thread nicely and break the pipe off inside the wall.

I should have told you to let the surplus water run out of the taps once you'd turned the water off, but seeing you're wet now anyway you can really get stuck into it. Shove a few socks and newspapers down the pipe while you try to separate the tap from the bit of pipe that came off with it.

About now the build-up of water pressure will blow the shower nozzle off and provide you with a rather nice little soap recess about five metres up the dining-room wall, and you should find there's a fairly impressive geyser in the middle of the street. This clears most of the deposit out of the pipes and the only way to obviate the possibility of a series of ginger feature walls is to position yourself between the pipes and the walls in question. Once the surplus water has run out, you can chip the wall away and bend the broken pipe around so that it points outside.

Now you can turn the water on again and swim around making notes on what you'd like the plumber to do when he arrives. You've done most of the groundwork, you might as well get a professional in to provide the finishing touches. Anyway, you'll need someone to help you clear up before having the place relined.

Going to the Races

Gidday. If you're going to maximise race-going you'll need to get dressed up well beyond the nines and you'll need a couple of things to carry; binoculars are very good as they help to act as a ballast later in the day when the wolves are howling. You park your car about 800 kilometres away in a carpark (which is Latin for 'expensive paddock') and by the time you get to the main buildings you should have built up a good thirst. Proceed directly to the bar. Do not pass go. Do not collect anything like $200.

Once you've had a few, you can move out to the gambling department and start whistling your fiscal toehold up the spout. The first race is easy. Anyone can pick the winner of the first race. The trouble with the first race is that no one's ever got there in time to bet on it. The first race finishes as you come out of the bar and the horse you were going to place your shirt on is on the board at a zillion to one and has just won the first race by ten lengths. Unfortunately in the second race you've got four gold-plated certainties all given to you by people who know the trainer's brother. So you stack your pfennigs on each of them for a win, and return to the bar and tell the barman you had the first race in your pocket if only you'd arrived early enough to bet on it. If his eyes glaze and he's obviously having trouble staying awake, don't worry, he probably had a late night or something.

If you go outside and peer through your binoculars now you'll see that there's a very big bloke standing right in front of you and if you listen carefully you'll overhear him telling someone that Mr Sandman will win the fifth race by a very long way indeed. So you shoot down and place a wager to that effect. Race Two has finished by now and the four nags you bet on had a great tussle in the run to the judge and eventually dead-heated for 17th. Race Three and Race Four seem to have gone, too. They always run Race Three and Race Four around the back somewhere and no one ever sees them, so you've got time for a couple of quick shots of juniper-extract before collecting on Race Five.

At this stage you'll run across a group of people you haven't seen for years because they've been in this bar together since shortly after the war. After a short time with your old friends you'll realise that the result of Race Five is not as important as the high harmony line in 'Shenandoah' and your day at the races begins to take on a new character.

People who care about placings, dividends and quinellas will suddenly seem a bit on the silly side and, providing you've cancelled everything on your books for about four days into the following week, you'll find that the only drawback of the whole thing is that the sport of kings is the father of the prince of hangovers.

Golf

Gidday. I'd like to have a few words with you about one of the most paradoxical leisure activities in the recorded annals. If it hadn't made the grade as a leisure activity it could easily have hit the headlines as a form of mentally debilitating torture. I refer, of course, to the royal and ancient business of golf and, if you're not up to a full-frontal lobotomy, then a round or two of golf is probably just what you're after.

It's not a very complicated game and if you can count up to about two or three you should find you'll be looked upon as something of a colossus out there on the sward.

You'll need a pair of two-tone dancing pumps with spikes in the soles. The spikes are put there especially by the designer to help you tell your golf shoes from your other shoes. You'll need a club, which is a stick with a knob on one end of it, and you'll need balls. There are 18 holes so, of course, you'll need at least 18 balls, although for the inexperienced golfer a bag of about 60 balls would appear to be the minimum requirement.

You step up to something called a tee, you place a ball on a little hatstand, and you give it a good lusty whack with your club. This should whip the little hatstand out from underneath and give you a good clear shot at the ball. You drive the ball as hard as you can down the fairway and you then follow it and hit it around in among the trees and across little ponds and through a lot of rather boring sandpits until eventually, of course, you lose the ball altogether.

By now you should be anything up to about 30 or 40 metres away from the actual tee where you started and it's time for phase two. You walk down the fairway towards the green. It's the walking you do in golf that makes it so good for you.

As you wander along the fairway you'll hear someone shout "fore". This means you've got a golf ball imbedded in your skull. Keep moving now because if you stop you'll seize up altogether. When you reach the green you take the flag out of the hole and say, "Here's looking at you, blue eyes". This is called a bogie and is considered pretty hot stuff by the bulk of the golfing fraternity. Then you proceed to the next tee and you whack another ball off down the fairway and the whole business is repeated. By the end of the round the 18 golf balls lodged in the back of your brain should have anaesthetised you to the point where you are no longer bothered by the unbridled tedium of the activity, your head is now worth about $45 on the open market and it's time to go.

If you like walking, a bit of physical exercise and the joy of competition, I recommend you have a very serious look at stamp collecting.

Playing a Musical Instrument

Gidday. As you'll know if you are musically inclined, the joy of playing an instrument is impossible to describe to anyone who has not spent most of what might otherwise have been a childhood locked in a room trying to spin straw into gold.

The first thing to work out is which musical instrument to play and as there is a fair to reasonable quorum of things to hit, pluck and blow down, this can look after a day or two in itself. Your best bet is to look for something you think you'd feel at home with and then actually go home and see how you feel without it. This will give you a fair idea of how silly you are, and you can choose an instrument accordingly. Of course there are some things that become obvious at a relatively early juncture. For instance in the normal run of events a four and a half thousand ton pipe-organ will be difficult to sequester away in the privacy of your own home and anyway if you feel like a bit of a fugue during the night whole suburbs can lift several feet off the ground and in most areas you need planning permission to play 'Chopsticks'. You'd be better with a less powerful instrument, like a flute for example, which is also handy for drain blockages.

In my carefully considered opinion though, the best thing to get hold of is our old friend the piano. You don't have to hold a piano up under your chin and there are very few better drinkstands. The only problem is how to actually play it. This is done as follows. Deal five cards to the piano and five to yourself. It's the piano's bid so hold your hand well up and look straight ahead. You should find after a few evenings you're winning more or less at will. I knew a bloke once who learned to play a whole orchestra. He made a bloody fortune.

A Dinner Party

Gidday. I'd like to have a word with you about having a dinner party and if you had one last night just stay where you are. Don't move. If you can find your mouth you might like to just practise saying your name a few times, although if that's going to involve the use of your tongue you'll probably have to go and take it out of the fridge and, if you can find the fridge, then you're on the improve and I must say it's nice to have you up and about again.

The first thing to decide when you're having a dinner party is what to eat, closely followed by where to eat it, how to eat it, what to drink, who to invite, who not to even mention it to, where to buy the food, what to wear and for how long, who to borrow things from and where you left the valium.

Let's just take these one at a time and subject them to analysis.

What to eat. Personally, I recommend a lemon meringue fondue with vichyssoise and a chop in it, followed by short long one-tonne nasi goreng and tomato sandwiches. As to where this should be actually consumed, I don't think you can go past a table. So put an extra leaf in the ironing board and use the chairs and the bathroom stool and the box the speakers came in and you'll be ready to serve.

The wines can be a bit of problem, as anyone who's ever had any will tell you, but fortunately there are guidelines laid down and if you follow these you'll be relatively safe.

If you're having fish, of course, you'll need a wine that complements taking millions of little bones out from behind your choppers and trying to sneak them down on to the plate in such a way that they don't keep sliding down into your pumpkin, so for that you'll need either a white wine or a red wine. You'd be very ill-advised to try anything else at this stage. Next, you'll need to consider a wine to go with a meat course, something that has a bit of body to it, and again I'd stick with red or white. Port is very pleasant in the post-prandial department or perhaps a liqueur or, better still, a little lie-down for a week or so.

As to what to wear, I don't think it matters much, as long as it's got enough zips and buttons that you can let it out about an acre and a half all round.

In the Bush

Gidday. I'd like to have a look at one of the great outdoor activities, and I'm referring here, of course, to the age-old business of tramping, or hiking, or bushwalking, or bush-sitting-down-and-resting, depending on how you feel about it.

The first thing to do is avail yourself of a certain amount of equipment, including a pair of good sturdy boots, so you can wear holes in your pair of good sturdy socks and get a comprehensive range of good sturdy blisters on your pseudopodia. You'll need a pack of some sort so that you can carry essential supplies into the unknown and drink them when your interest in endemic dicotyledons is flagging.

The main thing to remember before embarking on one of these little adventures is that at some stage you will get lost and when you get lost there are several cardinal rules to bear in mind or you'll remain lost, which is not a good thing to remain.

The first rule to take account of once you've achieved lostness is not to panic. You should ignore this rule. There's nothing wrong with a good panic. In fact, it's a cleansing experience and, if you can't go through a bit of good blind hysterical panic out in the sticks, where can you go? There are killjoys about, though, and you can't be too careful. Of course, if you don't panic, don't panic about it, you'll probably panic later.

There's probably someone in your party who knows how to use his watch as a compass and which berries are edible and how to light a fire with two pieces of dehydrated pizza. This person is called a natural leader and should be tied to a tree and ignored. The best thing to do is wait until night falls and then simply navigate your way home using the stars.

This is a fairly simple business and you don't have to know where the Panhandle is relative to due west. All you do is pick out some celestial landmark, Venus is a good one, and try to remember where it is relative to where you live. Then, of course, all you've got to do is keep walking until it's in that position and you'll be home. You might be a street or two out, but the blisters on your feet will have raised you to a height of about 90 metres above the houses and you should be able to make out the roof of your own residence and make your way towards it in your own time.

Duck-Shooting

Gidday. Now I'd like to have a bit of a natter with you about an activity known very loosely as duck shooting. I understand there are people about who believe that duck shooting is a somewhat barbaric caper involving the mass murder of the very beautiful winged quacking persons. This is quite simply a canard, as any restauranteur will tell you. I've known duck shooters, man and woman, all my life and I've never known one of them to even harm a duck, much less kill one. As a matter of fact I once heard of a bloke who claimed to have killed a duck when he hit it with the front of a fire engine but I think the fact that the duck had heel and toe plates and a number 9 1/2 stamped on it and to all intents and purposes appeared to be the world's first lace-up duck, may cast some doubt on the actual substance of the boast. The bloke actually gave his name as Napoleon, too, which gave his critics a fair bit of elbow-room.

The crucial semantic point to be ingested is that duck shooting means shooting *at* ducks, rather than actually shooting ducks. This is done as follows. You hide yourself away in a herbacious border somewhere so you can't be seen by anyone at all under any circumstances except from the air, by something like, say, for argument's sake, a duck. You aim your shotgun and you wait. The important thing at about this stage is the decoy. You have to give the duck the impression that you are actually yourself, personally, another duck.

There are two main methods of achieving duckhood. The first method is to fire the shotgun. This will break your shoulder off and fold both your arms neatly around your back in the manner made famous by wings. You'll fall backwards into the water and you will look and feel distinctly duckescent. The other thing to do, of course, is to sound like a duck, and for this there is a time-honoured device. You take a large bottle of whisky, remove the cap and suck on it very hard, drawing the liquid up into the body and making exactly the same sound that ducks make when they're having a few. Of course, in a twinkling of the first person you'll see ducks swooping about all over the place. And snakes. And in the fullness of time, elephants on bicycles.

Fortunately, though, duck shooting is a seasonal activity, which is a blessed relief to us all.

Sitting on the Beach

Gidday. For this you'll need a beach, which is a long sandy arrangement somewhere near the sea, and you'll need something to sit on.

First of all, you should mention to everyone that you're going to just get away from things and let the wind blow away the cobwebs. Then go and find a beach with about a million people on it. If you're going to get away from it all you'll need to keep an eye on it all so you can keep your distance. Find yourself a piece of beach and get out your towel.

In front of all these people, and some of them were queuing on Thursday night for this, you've got to get out of your clothes and into your beach clobber.

Wrap the towel around yourself and slowly fumble away underneath trying to remove things as they come to hand, pulling each item out from under the towel and hiding it under some previous marginally less embarrassing item. And keep an eye on those people behind in case they rush you.

After a while things should be getting a bit sparse underneath, and about now you should break into a kind of carefree lunatic whistle to carry you over the last stages. When you've got down to the stage between phase one and Bob's your uncle, reach over and get your swimming gear, being careful not to move too rapidly or clap your hands above your head. You pull on your natty little summer sartorials and, with as much nonchalance as you can muster, you whip the towel away to reveal yourself, resplendent in beach wear, with the outfit on back to front and both legs down one leg hole. Don't let this worry you, just sit down fairly smartly and survey the scene.

While you were whistling, a gross of wet canines have come over and with any luck they'll shake about 400 litres of ocean all over you. This will cool you down nicely and you'll be ready for a bit of sunbathing.

Lie on your stomach and open a book. The book isn't for reading and it'll get sand all through it so take a book you don't want but one with a good title. If Tolkien had knocked out something on Wagner it would've been just the job. The sun will play about your person and the glare from the book will make sure your face gets plenty of good hot blinding rays and it'll reflect off that cream on your nose and you'll get some impression of what it must have been like to lose to Joe Louis after drinking Harvey Wallbangers for a fortnight.

My advice at about this stage is to go for a walk. Remember this is not just any old walk, this is a beach walk so you'll have to do your special unselfconscious body-beautiful casual stroll. Fix your eyes on the horizon and command your body into position A. If the beach is fairly long you can relax every now and then and have a bit of a slouch but if it's relatively short and heavily peopled you'll need to hold yourself in the same position for the entire performance, so get comfortable and if anyone looks at you, just flex a couple of ripples and look as sensitive as you can without actually laughing.

By the time all this is over you'll need a lie down and you can have a bit of a look at other people walking up and down. Then it'll be your turn again. After each completed stroll, as you return to your towel, the judges will hold up the score cards, the lowest score is dropped and the average of the remainder is flashed up on a big electronic board behind the car park. If you want to save your big effort for the nationals, my advice is to whip away home as soon as you've notched up a personal best.

The Tip

Gidday. Now there's one thing I'd like to clear up straight away and that is the common misconception that a tip is a place where you take stuff, unload the stuff, and then proceed to belt off home devoid of stuff. This is incorrect. I don't know who puts these things about but they're not true. A tip is quite simply a place where you take stuff, unload the stuff, wander about for a while kicking pre-war *Women's Weekly*s and manifold gaskets, then load up with new stuff, about half a tonne more than you came with, and then it's off home for unloading and arguments.

If it were just a place for dumping stuff there wouldn't be room to move for stuff, but it's not; it's a redistribution centre, from each according to his ability, to each according to his need. And by this process stuff is constantly diffused through society and an old chair that you've had for 200 years and can't stand anymore goes off to the tip and bingo, by Monday lunchtime it's been snaffled by a vanload of rebellious middle-class children and it's for sale at $1000 as a mock-rococo lampshade. So whatever you've got lurking around in a back corner of a gardening shed, no matter how useless it seems to you, there's probably a bloke down at the tip tossing old shoes into a puddle just hoping someone's going to come along with one in precisely that colour. And you should see what he's got. He's got a whole trailer-load of goodies and right in the middle of it, between the 75 kilometres of fishing tackle he got caught round the oar and the box of tennis rackets someone left in the sun and which for the last few years have been serving due west, right in the middle of all this is one of those things you've been after for ages, a doover for one of those things that clamps on the back of the number you first thought of.

Your best idea is to pack up the lunch dishes and whip off to the tip. In fact, take the lunch dishes with you; I know for a fact there's a bloke down there with a kitchen sink.

Bringing Work Home

Gidday. I'd like to address our attention today to the activity known as bringing work home. This is an under-rated time-waster and is often erroneously referred to as being somehow connected to the work that's not brought home. This misconception is dangerous and should be nipped in the bud.

Firstly, you should get somewhere good and central, like the dinner table, and empty about 50 kilograms of old biros and manila folders and bus tickets on to it. Re-arrange the room to fit in with your new purpose and sit down at the table. When you start sorting things out a bit you'll find you've got to use bits of the floor to augment your filing system. You should have enough work for about 18 months stashed around you in a semi-circle and perhaps a small ladder for getting in and out.

It should be dinnertime and you'll have to clear a small space for the prandials, making sure that all your very urgent and important work is on the top so it can be covered in gravy and lettuce. After dinner you'll have to give any children in the district a biro and a few hundred sheets of paper due to their tendency when confronted with stationery to become artists, letter-writers and paper-hangers.

Place a sheet of paper in front of you, pick up a pen and look out the window. This will cause the baby to cry. Montessori noticed this in the thirties but it's a lesson you'll have to learn for yourself. Placing the baby on one knee, you begin working, putting the pen on the face of the paper and drawing a very long line across it as the baby whips the paper away and eats it. While you're removing wood pulp from the mouth of the progeny, try to think of something you can do that doesn't involve writing. The other kids have finished the first section of their art folios by now and are ready to show you pictures of princesses and trees and houses and trains and snowmen and things. At about this stage the baby's face will suddenly be coloured in with a pen you thought was in your pocket and you'll notice you've got water on the knee and it's time to change the baby's tweeds. Actually, it's beginning to look as if this is the only thing you'll get done all evening because the other deductions are coming in off a ten pace run and long-jumping into your filing system.

The best idea at this point is to pack up anything that's not covered in tooth marks and pop it back into the bag for another day. The only good thing about the whole performance is that you get more done like this than you do at the office.

Skiing

Gidday. I'd like to have a word or two with you today about an activity that is enjoying its customary seasonal popularity even as I speak, and I refer here, of course, to skiing, which is a very old pastime and deservedly so, in my view.

Skiing was discovered by a Swiss gentleman during the middle ages. (I think he was about 45.) He lived up the Matterhorn and he fell over one night while putting the cat out. He also discovered the skijump, the somersault, the avalanche and the greenstick fracture in the clavicle.

Nowadays, of course, skiing has become available to pretty well anyone in society with a thirst for adventure and about $100,000. Mind you, since its advent as a purely sportive activity, it has garnered unto its person several new characteristics. One important innovation that has been made is the discovery that being up a mountain can cause a severe dryness in the mouth. This can be alleviated only by drinking, which can cause a severe dryness in the mouth, and so it goes on.

Consequently, the skis became larger and longer to give the celebrants a better chance of remaining in the vertical, although later on they were given a pair of sticks to help steady them in cases of wind and believe you me hot wine can be very problematical in that respect.

In severe cases a large full length white leg casing is placed on the skier and with that, plus the skis, plus the sticks, it's practically impossible to fall over, even if you're preserved in alcohol.

Now, of course, there are some people who do actually glide about on the snow, but this is a very dangerous business and should be avoided. I take it we're all familiar with the concept of a mountain, which is a tall arrangement made of rock. Because of the cold at the top of these things, snow and ice are frequently spotted amassing on the outer surface, or epiderm. What some of these people do is slide down the slippery outer covering of the mountain until they get to the bottom. This, of course, is insane and therefore extremely popular, particularly with people who've done well in aircraft components and cost accounting.

Tennis

Gidday. Now today I want to waylay you with another suggestion about how to show the weekend who's boss. This method is safe, completely dependable and fulfils most of the requirements of a leisure activity as laid down in the Geneva Convention. It is time-consuming to a point where you can actually think you're busy, it's tiring, it involves special clothing and equipment and in general terms it's a 100 per cent bona fide waste of time within the meaning of the Act. I refer, of course, to the ancient and revered art of tennis.

First of all, you'll need a tennis court and, if you play your cards right, you can spend till about Sunday lunchtime waiting for one to be vacated by three or four big Brunhildes who've been whacking around on it since April, rallying for service.

By the time you get a court it'll be raining and there'll be a Force 9 blowing leaves and silt in from Asia. This will carry the ball over the net, the wire fence and a 15-hectare subdivision at the back. The net will have wound itself into a thin line of black string, so you can't tell whether your shots are going under it or over it, and you only find out where it is when you hurl yourself forward to smash a lob and it bends you over in the trousers and drops you on your back between the tramlines.

You should really wear whites and have a good racquet but, if you couldn't raise a mortgage in time, you can generally get away with an honest attempt. A pair of white shorts you once washed with some red curtains and now have a blotchy pink aspect to them and a painting rag with armholes is often quite acceptable, if you've got shoes the same colour and a good hat. A good hat is crucial and, if you can't get one of those visor arrangements from an old New York newspaper editor, you might get by with a sweatband, which is like a sock you wear round your bonce to keep your brains from sliding out your ears. Always remember that the best sports gear has two stripes down it, so whatever you've got, get a good thick biro and plant a couple of stripes on it so you look like a pre-war postman and you'll be OK in the sartorial department.

The next thing is the game and. although it's the least important aspect of the whole exercise, it's as well to know a couple of the basic rules in case the Rosewalls on the next court ask you whether their last serve was a let or an inwards one-and-a-half with a degree of difficulty of 2.4.

The way to score is relatively simple and once you've played a few games, you'll pick it up, no trouble. The first person serves, which is called a double-fault, and so it goes on until you get to the point where all the balls are in the blackberries up behind the carpark. Then the person to the left of the dealer says "juice" and you all go and do that. From memory it's fun from there on.

Writing an Autobiography

Gidday. Now I'd like to have a few words with you today about writing an autobiography.

This is a highly recommended form of leisure activity, as it takes up large chunks of time and, if you're a slow writer or you think particularly highly of yourself, you can probably whistle away a year or two. A cursory glance at most autobiographies available on the open market will convince you that they were written to fill in a bit of time.

If you feel that your life hasn't really been as fascinating as it might have been, don't let it worry you. If you reckon you've had a dull patch, say you didn't do much of any great moment between about 1900 and last Wednesday, don't be downhearted. All you've got to do is make it up. Pad it out a bit. You'll get away with it if you remember the cardinal rules of autobiography.

Always take issue with Ruskin on a couple of minor points. Any points will do. And if you don't know what Ruskin said, don't worry, neither does anyone else. It's not important to know what he said. Just remember to take issue with him.

Always mention your travels. Say how impressed you were on first seeing the Alps, or the Moors, or a few cathedrals, or a famous gallery somewhere. Or if you want to be an iconoclast, say how unimpressed you were. But somehow you've got to work in your impressions one way or another. If you've never actually seen the Alps, there are photos of them everywhere. Have a look and see what you think.

Always spend a fair bit of time mulling over the title. Titles are very important and you can't be too careful. Puns are very good titles of course, and very bad puns are extremely good. Make a list of excruciating puns and the ones you reject will do you very nicely as chapter headings. Another favourite is a piece of Shakespeare or some other literature of great profundity. Always use half a line, never a complete quotation. Something like "Prithee nuncle whist lo my leige waits without" is no good at all, but "'Prithee nuncle whist", "Prithee nuncle whist lo", "whist lo my leige'", "lo my leige waits", "'my leige waits without" or just plain "Prithee nuncle" are all crackers.

The only thing you need now is photographs. Photographs give a life substance and are a handy device for separating the front part of the book from the back part. You'll need a few photos of your family and you should leave these in the oven overnight in a mixture of cold tea and aircraft glue so they have about them the requisite appearance of the tranquil days of yore.

You'll need one photo of yourself with someone famous (and by famous I mean more famous than you). You'll need a couple of shots of buildings, one of a picnic and, of course, one of the Alps. So as you can see, it's not a difficult business and remember this is also your big opportunity to explain what a wonderful person you are and how you've been consistently misunderstood by your friends and mentors and most of all by riffraff like Ruskin and the Alps.

Yachting

Gidday. I'd like to wave my dulcets about today on a subject of major fascination for all leisure-minded people, and I'm referring here, of course, to yachting. Yachting is a well-established method of putting a weekend under your belt and it has the added advantage of causing total lack of recall. Whole slabs of your life can become complete blanks.

There are several basic requirements in this area and it's as well to be familiar with the conventions and the terminology if you are going to spend any amount of time before the mast.

Firstly, you'll need a white polo-neck jumper and a short yellow nylon raincoat, preferably one with a few badges sewn up the arm. This should get you into any yacht club and, if your income is over about $15,000 a week, you should be able to hold your own in conversation until you pick up the vernacular and feel completely at home.

You'll have to know the difference between starboard and port, of course. Port is a rather furry beverage and I think starboard is made from gin and crème de menthe. The starboard side is where the gin is kept and Port Said is a place in North Africa. If anyone mentions Port Said you're a fair bit out of your way and you probably won't be in the office until well after smoko on the Monday.

The mast is a tall arrangement in the middle for steadying yourself against and the sails are a series of big sheets that indicate the wind direction so you can lean into the updraft and prevent yourself from being washed away.

If the wind changes dramatically someone will tell you to 'go about', which simply means turning yourself around and toasting the land out the other side.

'Lee O' means everyone has to down whatever they're drinking and have whatever the captain's having.

The 'bow' is a mixture of rum and cloves and Malvern water, and a 'stern' is a little bit like a black Russian with a dash of retsina. To 'splice' something is to add lemon. An 'upper fore mizzen tops'l halyard' is a gin sling with a small piece of rope in it and a 'cleat' is a nip of gin taken straight out of bottle cap with nothing added.

That's really about all you'll need to know at this stage; not many novices can last much longer than a few starboards, a couple of sterns and a cleat or two and, if you splice the upper fore mizzen tops'l halyard, it'll all be over in the first round.

Anyway, give it a go and, if you don't take to yachting the first time you try it, there are plenty of places you can go to dry out.

THE PROBLEM OF KNOWLEDGE

One of Mr Dagg's many concerns was ideas themselves.
How are we to understand the world we live in? What do we mean when
we say things? And if so, why? What is the matter with our education
system and would it help if we had one?
(Let's not always see the same hands.)

The Socratic Paradox

Gidday. I'd like to have a word or two with you about the Socratic Paradox, which, without being too technical about it, is a paradox worked out by the late Socrates in order to explain some of the pitfalls involved in explaining things.

The argument says in essence that you can't learn things you don't already know, and given the widely accepted view that there's some difficulty to be encountered in trying to learn something you do already know, I'm afraid it's beginning to look as if the whole business of learning is largely overrated and should probably be left alone.

I personally have always held this to be more or less self-evident, although unfortunately my reasoning turns out to be a good deal less Platonic than I had hoped. Socrates argued that if you don't know something you probably wouldn't recognise the knowledge if it popped up in your porridge. And if you did recognise it then in some sense you must already have had the knowledge beforehand. And that, therefore, learning is merely a process whereby we recollect knowledge that is already in us.

This, of course, touches on the Fred Dagg Theory of the Human Memory and even though Socrates doesn't, so far as I know, have any real right of reply in the matter any more, there are just one or two points I'd like to clear up.

Firstly, if the knowledge is in there anyway, at what stage was it put there and whose job is it to go about the place feeding knowledge in through people's ears before the memory takes over and renders the whole thing academic? As a matter of fact, I knew a bloke once who thought we were all born with a certain number of words in us and when we talked them out, we died, which impressed me as being fundamentally sound until I found out that he thought "Portia Faces Life" was the story of a woman named Portia Face.

This knowledge represented the recollection of something I don't think Socrates has made enough allowance for, and that is that lack of knowledge or the knowledge of things that aren't quite right can be recalled just as easily and in some cases more easily than good solid everyday stuff like coming in out of the rain.

It's also possible to forget things and then forget that you've forgotten them. And then if you can recall the fact that you've forgotten something does this necessarily qualify as knowledge?

As a matter of fact I'll try and get back to you on this one. I'm a little bit confused at the moment and it's nearly time for my tablet.

The Perils of Air

Gidday. I presume you're all well aware, in fact it's my devout hope that you're acutely aware that I don't want to be alarmist about this. But, on the other hand, there's no point in hiding behind a bushel and pretending everything's perfectly all right when really we all know very well it isn't.

I've warned you off the bicycle, which I always thought was only a passing phase anyway, and I've recently revealed in the public forum the horrifying dangers of lip gas; and with any real luck you're now philosophically prepared for the startling disclosure that getting up in the morning can kill.

I'll tell you basically how this happens. There's no point in going into it too deeply as it's actually a little bit frightening and needless scientific detail will probably serve only to worry you. You will appreciate that during the night, as we scientists call it, the atmosphere has a chance to settle down. During the day it is subjected to the injection of industrial fumes, germs, toxic gases and, on occasions, balloons; and during the night it sorts itself out into basic elements, hydrogen, nitrogen, earth, fire and water. And in order to do this it requires absolute absence of artificial stimulus; the wind is all right, the process can cope with wind, wind is a natural force and as such is an integral part of the wonderful jigsaw of microscopic life, but the movement of people through the realigning gases while they're actually in the process of realignment is extremely dangerous.

This is why people who come home at half-past four in the morning look so terrible the following day. The realignment has been disturbed by the passage of their bodies and has wrought a terrible havoc upon their persons, particularly around the eyes and in the back of the mouth. Any movement, and getting up in the morning is a good example, disturbs the natural regrouping of the gaseous elements and, instead of walking into a fresh revitalised atmosphere, you're likely to stroll into a big pocket of incomplete air, and the effects of this are horrendous. I've done it several times. The lungs and the spleen are the first to go, and after that you'll be all over the place.

Stay in bed, that's my advice to you, and if possible stay asleep.

The Meaning of Life
Transcript of a Broadcast to the Nation - September 24th, 1977

Gidday. I think this is a particularly significant occasion and it seems eminently suitable that we should ignore very briefly the peripheral areas, however valuable in the wonderful tapestry of science, and I think we should have a crack at addressing ourselves instead to the perpetual cosmic giant-killer, the question "What is life?" It's been worrying scientists for thousands of years; mind you they're a jumpy bunch of garçons your science boys and they do tend to worry very easily and I feel that the very least we can do is to spend a few moments of our valuable time in quiet and restful contemplation as to what it's all about and why we're here. And then after that we can have some lunch.

As to the business of when life actually got going there's very little argument among the lads who are working in that area; of course some of them are getting on a bit now and the smallest upset would have them toppling into the afterlife so they do like to sit around and agree with one another and knock off the departmental port. The actual day of the beginning of life is not known because, of course, the National Geographic was in a very adumbral phase at that stage. It is known though and generally agreed by the boys that, if the first man who ever lived were alive today he'd be pulling around about $47 million a week in old-age pensions.

There have been several old boys located in various spots. For instance, there was Bogman, who was located in a bog. We don't actually know what he was doing in the bog but he was located there. Science slowly, with the help of these discoveries, is piecing together the story of man's evolution and there seems very little doubt that man is descended from Neanderthal primates, as we scientists call them, or, in lay terms, Mummy and Daddy.

Of all the many turning points and crucial stages from primitive ape-like creatures through to the sophisticated and marginally less primitive ape-like creatures that you see about you at zoos and football matches, the most curious development of all is that of the human brain. The human brain has got man into a lot more trouble than has previously been supposed and, unless we come up with some way of putting the brain out of commission or obviating some of the more ludicrous effects of the brain, I don't think life's going to get any better.

The main shortcoming of the human brain is that it has led to all this discussion about the meaning of life, which is not really very healthy. It's quite a dangerous business because the more you think about life, the less likely you are to reach a conclusion; that is if you don't count concluding that you aren't going to reach a conclusion as an actual conclusion.

Now of all the attempts to work out what life is actually about, one of the more interesting ones comes from the boys who reckoned you don't know anything. You can't know stuff, these guys reckoned, because when you think about it, and you'll just have to accept the term 'think about it' there until the man arrives with the official phrase book, all your so-called knowledge about the world is based on your perceptions and your perceptions are just a touch more fallible than people have cared to admit.

You are here talking about Bishop Berkeley and the solipsists, of course.

Yes, Bishop Berkeley, whose brother I believe is the captain of India.

It has been suggested by the Bishop that you can't know things because your perceptions are notoriously fallible. For instance, the visual sense has been known to play tricks. Sometimes when you think you see something you actually don't see it and sometimes you don't see something, or you say you don't see it, and it's common knowledge around the village that you saw it. And, of course, that can lead to trouble. You can't go drawing any conclusions, this is what these garçons reckon, from that sort of thing or you'll make a monkey of yourself in open court. This is what the Bishop reckoned and this argument applies to all the senses.

Samuel Johnson who was a kind of . . . well he was fat, let's face it, he was a fat person; he reckoned that he cleaned up the problem one day when he kicked a stone and he stated with relative certainty that he was rewarded with a goodly sharp pain belting through his bunion. Now, of course, you could say that Samuel only thought he kicked the stone, when in fact he was actually home in bed eating cumquats and thinking up some one-liners for a 21st speech he was writing for Saturday.

The whole business of doubt was perfected and refined a little later on by a character named René Descartes, who was a member of the French nation, and after he'd finished with it there wasn't a whole lot of mileage left in it and the up-and-coming apprentice thinkers decided to give the whole area a swerve and get on to something with a bit more class where they could show off a bit better. What René did was he started doubting things. Now once you start doubting your perceptions you get on to realising that you can't be sure whether you're actually here or maybe you only think you're here, which is a bit of a worry, and it's only a matter of moments before you're picking spots of light off the wall and putting them in a basket and pretty soon you'll find yourself in a tight white overcoat in a room full of Napoleons and Lord Nelsons, which is the principal fallacy of René's idea.

Of course in the 20th century we have produced a fair array of theories about what life is actually about and probably the existentialists take the buttered confection for thinking they had it all worked out. They used to hang about around the Paris area, which is in what we used to call 'Gaul', before the Pyrrhics. They talked about how terrible life was and how they didn't know if they'd get to the weekend. They reckoned life was a pretty dreadful business and was filled with a thing called 'ennui'. 'Ennui' is a terrible thing that seems to have roughly the same effect as terminal boredom. 'Ennui' actually is a French word meaning 'Henry', and the story goes that once you get a touch of the Henries it's all down hill and the only way to relieve the symptoms is to whip down to the harbour and pull a wave over your bonce and call it a day.

From these examples you can see the dangers of thinking too much about what life is about and whether or not it's worth living.

I have studied most of the better known theories and if I understand them at all, which is a pretty dubious proposition, and if I'm here at all, and again there is some doubt, not to mention cold water being thrown on that at the present point in time, I must say that they're not really very helpful, all these theories. Not really very helpful at all.

A mate of mine, a bloke named Bruce Bayliss who's lived up the road from us ever since he moved in, reckons that he exists. He's quite positive that he exists. And if he doesn't exist, he reckons, why does he have to pay tax?

He reckons that, even though he does get the Henries a bit now and again at the end of the financial year, he's convinced that he's here and, if some people reckon that they're not here, then that's fine with Bruce and they can buy their own beer.

He seems to, in his terms at least, have dispensed more or less completely with the traditional worries about his own existence although there are those who claim that Bruce is a wee bit closer to the simian primates than most people reckon. Bruce is called a naive realist and I don't know that he's not right, myself. I've seen a few existentialists in my time, I've been to funerals, and they don't seem anywhere near as happy about things as Bruce does. And if we're all imagining we're here until we imagine we've bitten the dust then I think it's a lot easier on the wife and kids if we imagine ourselves to be a bit happy about it.

I'm not suggesting we become like Bruce. It wouldn't do to revert completely to being chimps. But somewhere between Bruce and the rest of the scientific world there lurks a workable hypothesis that I reckon we should all get our teeth into.

Whither Education?

Gidday. In the great debate about education, it is important to know what the education system is supposed to produce, so we can assess other things by relating them to the model and drawing comparisons so that we can lay down guidelines, general parameters, rough outlines, working briefs and topics for discussion.

In order to assist in the discussion and perhaps pave the way for tomorrow's leaders, I have decided to make myself available as an example of what education can do.

When I was born, I realised pretty well immediately that I knew very little. This worried me and I went about the laborious business of acquiring knowledge with a passion rarely seen in the post-war era. And out of my many years' schooling I learnt the following things.

- The capital of Peru is either Lima or Lisbon, and the one that isn't, is the capital of either Norway or Oslo.
- If you want to multiply something by 11, you add the numbers together and put the answer in the middle. For instance 34 x 11 is 374. But if it adds up to more than 10, like 96 x 11 would, then you'd have to take the answer away from something and I'm not actually sure what you'd have to take it away from.

- People look fairly silly if you sneak up behind them and belt them very hard in the back of the knees.
- My auntie's pen is on the table.
- "Earth has not anything to show more fair
  Dull would he be of soul who could pass by
  A sight so touching in its majesty
  Ships, towers, something or other and steeples and things
  Lie open unto the fields and the sky
  The ploughman homeward plods his weary way
  The something or other fearful symmetry"
- "John Gilpin was a citizen of credit and renown
  A trainband captain eke was he"
- The (whole lot of things beginning with g) Limpopo River, is an extremely good example of something or other.
- I before E except after C.
- Amo amas amat, amamus abismus abonghole.
- Osmosis is the passage of something or other through something or other else; a semipermeable membrane, I think, although what that might be I shudder to think.
- You always sign yourself "Yours faithfully" at the end of a business letter, which is, of course, a letter to a coal company. And you used to actually write your address and the date so that they sloped down on a bit of an angle, but I think that's been phased out now with decimalisation or something.
- Nylon stockings are made out of coal, somehow, although how they do it I can't quite remember. It's all to do with carbon bonding, which is mixed up with organic chemistry somehow. The name of a substance in organic chemistry tells you how many carbon bonds it contains. Ethane's got two I think. Two, lumps I suppose, of coal, for every, perhaps, gallon of water, I suppose, although what the exact formula for stockings is I don't know.
- When a frog is dissected, if you pick out a spot on the floor and just look at it and think of a football match or something, you'll probably get through it without being sick. No one else will notice you. They've all picked spots off on the wall or the scalpel or the back of someone's head. Don't worry about it, you'll be jake.
- Two of the most important aspects of *Pride and Prejudice*, by Jane Austen, and

they have very great bearing on the question, are pride and prejudice. Pride as exemplified in somebody or other, and prejudice, which is personified by somebody or other else. (Darcy rings a bit of a bell or the Great White Whale or someone, I can't be sure.)

- Photosynthesis is a process whereby plants convert energy from the sun, which is light, I suppose, into pollen, I think.

- Czar Alexander, or Nicholas, the First or the Second or maybe the Third (I think there were three Alexanders), emancipated the serfs in eighteen hundred and something or other. The year 1861 springs to mind but maybe that was when my brother had his tonsils out.

- Abraham Lincoln had a black beard and was found in a log cabin in some bulrushes somewhere and he said that democracy was government by the people, of the people and for the people, which we know from our Latin means that democracy is either dative or ablative, or possibly something else. And Lincoln was assassinated in a theatre by somebody Booth, who might have had something to do with the Salvation Army or he could have been the bloke who founded the telephone box. I'm not quite sure.

- Aside from Lincoln, just about everyone in history died of syphilis, although there are one or two notable exceptions; Shelley (whose wife wrote *Starwars* or something), he drowned, and Joan of Arc of course, who was shot for spying during the First World War.

- Sound moves about the place in the form of waves. I don't know why. It just does. There are short waves and long waves and even the very occasional tearful farewell. And they travel faster than light waves. No that's right, that's wrong, they travel slower than light waves. Light travels faster than sound, except after C. And they can bounce off certain objects these sound waves and this would appear to account for echoes. Of course they bounce better off some objects than off others. They don't bounce very well off carpet. But good examples of things they bounce off very nicely indeed, include tiled bathrooms, tunnels under railway stations, deserted grandstands and Her Majesty's Opposition.

Now, as a matter of fact, I've got a letter here from a person who claims to have learned a whole lot of things at school that I've not only never heard of but, in some cases, I find totally unacceptable.

For starters this character informs me that the way to calculate the distance around a circle is πR. I'm not saying this is completely insane but, on the other hand, I'm not sure that I can go along with it either. It just seems too silly for me. As if anyone would want to know the distance around a circle anyway, and what R might be I'm wily enough not to ask, and if π really is $^{22}/_7$ I want to know why. I'm not prepared to just accept these things on trust. "Question everything" I was always told, and when I did I was encouraged to continue my inquiries while doing my justly famous impression of a staple in the boss's office.

Anyway, I don't see why this character isn't prepared to find the distance around a circle by the time-honoured method of adding up the cosine of the sum of the squares on the other two sides.

As if that's not bad enough I'm then informed that on the bridge at Avignon, everyone dances all around. Now this I'm not going to argue with. This is just crazy enough to be true. But the statement "C'est magnifique mais ce n'est pas la guerre", which according to me means "it is magnificent but it is not the railway station", seems to me to be entirely pointless, and if this is what new maths is on about then label me a fuddy-duddy and put me to one side thank you very much.

The thing I really draw the line at though is the proposition that "the distances travelled by a body moving with a uniformly accelerating velocity are to one another as the squares of the time." This is just nonsense. They aren't at all. I don't know what they are but I'll bet they're not that. I might be wrong, of course, I was away the day they did science. Anyway, you've all been very good so you can go home early today. Toodle whom.

Television Sport

1983–1985

Australian Farnarkeling Back in Business

Finland. Wednesday.

Last night the national side staged an amazing comeback to retrieve the fat from the fire at the last minute in the second half of injury time in the group 1 quarterfinals of the European Championships being played at the indoor farnarkeling centre in Helsinki late last night Australian time.

The Australians came from 15 arkles 2 tackles and a bracket-and-a-half down, to get up off the paving and defeat the highly credentialled and very well-performed Scotland who are ranked second in the world and haven't been beaten on a European grommit in nearly four years.

The Australian side, undermanned since its much-vaunted backline drove a small catering van into a water hazard at a charity equestrian event on Saturday, has had it all to do since arriving here for the European campaign. Already troubled by lack of form in recent outings and in particular by lack of drive in the centre where both Graeme Graham and the evergreen Dave Sorenson have been sidelined, Graham with extenuated shoulder ligaments and Sorenson with a corked thigh, the team arrived in Budapest a fortnight ago to find that their equipment was sitting on the runway at Broome airport due to a filing error.

When it arrived two days later it was found that the material in some of the flukems and the outside ends of the boot-wefting had been altered by exposure to temperatures in excess of the boiling point of some of the carpet nails used in the construction of the upper sections of the transom-housing. Replacement equipment was sent for but, as far as team officials were aware when I spoke to them a few minutes ago, it isn't here yet. Australia went into last night's affair with most of their gear borrowed from the Canadians and with the dorsal hinges and much of the scrotal padding borrowed from the South Koreans.

In the event it was nip and tuck all evening, Australia mounting good attacks, principally up the right wing where Neville Dorf was as fluent as we've ever seen him, and in the centre where thrust was coming from Lo Bat, the Chinese boy from Port Adelaide. Australia's finishing was not good, however, and too many opportunities went begging to arkle from quite handy positions. It wasn't until Plinth was taken from the grommit with what looked very much like a nasty knot in the clavicle that Australia began to regroup up front and go about the business of actually building a total.

Dave Sorenson is one of the great converters of the post-war era, although he hasn't arkeled at the top level for quite a few seasons now and when he was dragged out of retirement for this tournament there were plenty of those who thought he'd never be able to keep up with the modern game and when he came on last night just before the umlaut, I have to say he looked in all sorts of trouble. He was slow. He was sluggish. At one stage he tried to turn while moving laterally across the back of the cotyledan and if he hadn't run into the side of one of the hospitality tents he may well have sustained permanent damage to the entire upper part of his person. This seemed to steady him, however, and within moments he began to arkle with all the authority of a master. He notched up three or four absolute beauties before the Scottish coach shifted Fergusson and put the Quinn brothers in around Sorenson like a blanket. In the next six minutes Sorenson arkled 15 times and took Australia from nine behind to full of running and in front by two. It was this passage of play that altered the nature of the fixture and, although Scotland jumped away again in the latter stages, Sorenson pulled one out from well behind the tripod and the Quinn brothers, who must have thought they had him, were completely outflanked. By the time they looked up the gonad had reached its cruising height and there were Australians all over the ground swinging towels round their heads and enhancing the air with well-meaning obscenities.

Perhaps out of this Australia have sensed that this thing is possible over here. They withstood wave after wave of attack in extra time to hold the plucky Caledonians out and they looked a very determined outfit at the after-match function.

The cost of this victory might well prove to be catastrophic. Tragically, Dave Sorenson may take no further part in proceedings following an unfortunate incident on full time when he arkeled successfully but lost control while attempting a reverse Hasselblad and caught part of his lower mandible on a heating fan. Surgeons are non-committal about his condition but are apparently quietly confident they can get him down out of the roofing by Friday.

Australians Hit their Straps

Korea. Thursday.

The Australian Farnarkeling Team gave every indication on Friday night that it might be running into form at the business end of the season as it accounted for Italy in a majestic and confidence-building first-round display at the World Championships being contested in somewhat balmy conditions under lights here in Seoul.

The programme for Australia's defence of the bevelled orb has been the subject of some scepticism in recent months as the troubled national squad has registered a string of lack-lustre performances against often boisterous but fundamentally inferior opposition sides drawn principally from the rest of the world.

When they arrived in Seoul there were immediately problems. The hotel had double-booked four floors and there was no possibility of getting in anywhere else as the whole town was packed to the gunwhales and it was past three in the morning. Ian Geddes and Stewie Davidson slept in a telephone booth in the hotel carpark. Neville Dorf spent his first night on foreign soil in a goods lift with his feet in the ashtray and his head in a potted plant. Dave Sorenson, whose pelvic brace wasn't due to come off until the Thursday, slept standing up in the foyer and woke in some surprise to find that he was holding nearly two dozen umbrellas and a fair range of gentleman's millinery.

It was a somewhat bedraggled sight which met the eyes of team management as they arrived for breakfast fresh from a working session on threats from some of the Western Bloc countries to pull out of the Championships unless the playing surface at the Hyperbowl was changed.

There had actually been suggestions as late as mid-morning Thursday that the Astro-Arkle© surface, which is not universally favoured by the players, might be replaced by Flexi-Gromme©, the rather more spongy substance developed by the Swedes in order to cope with variations in temperature and atmospheric pressure.

In the event, organisers decided that the surface was playable as it was and the festivities got under way at the appointed time as per the attractively designed brochure.

The Italians began confidently and displayed their traditionally well-balanced combination of strength and speed with perhaps a slight tendency to waste opportunities out wide where Bartocelini was giving away a metre or two to the rapidly improving Graeme Graham and where Australia consistently found an overlap by running one player through the bracket and another down the back of the shifting tube. There were seldom fewer than three Australians to the left of the hassleblad and by the mid-point of the second warble Sorenson was arkeling with ominous authority. The Italians made a surprising tactical error shortly after the umlaut by concentrating their defensive effort on the unlikely Dorf. Dorf had intercepted a pass from Martinetti to Rossi and the Italians obviously assumed the interception to have been intentional. As far as Coach Donnatesto was concerned, Dorf was the dangerman. This left Graeme Graham to roam the circle and he fed Sorenson with good gonad until Boreo was shifted forward and the Italian reassessment of Dorf began to make its presence felt.

Australia had the fixture parcelled-up by that stage, however, and it was encouraging to see the defensive operation knitting together so well after all the problems of recent months.

The next encounter will be with either Peru or the Ross Dependencies who saw Denmark off in an elegant affair late on Wednesday. Unfortunately, Sorenson pulled a bank of lockers down on top of himself while grabbing for his towel in the ablutions facility and it will be another few days before the power of speech is revouchsafed and he can comment on his condition. Australia can ill-afford to be without him for long in this class of competition.

Australian Farnarkeling at Crossroads

Colombo. Monday.

Australian farnarkeling was rocked to its foundations this week. On Tuesday, a seemingly aimless Australian side containing no fewer than seven of the World Championship players was humiliated for three warbles by the Zambian Under-19s, and only a purple-patch from the still-injured Sorenson prevented the team from bowing out of the competition altogether and heading homewards before the commencement of the second round. It was an unfortunate exhibition, and some very serious thinking is necessary at selector level if further catastrophe is to be averted.

The Australians were especially poor in defence, which allowed the agile Zambians (particularly Kwee) to carve out huge tracts of territory at will, operating from the centre and exercising complete control of the flanks. And big Stewie Davidson must be wondering why he came here. He was left standing by little Ngawa, and the only thing he did properly all afternoon was consume half an orange.

Other big name players to be completely eclipsed were Leslie Stavridos, Robin Wylie and Neville Dorf. On one memorable occasion, Dorf had only to stroke the gonad slightly forward of his own feet in order to set up a cascading Widdershins Pincer involving three players and salvaging a tincture of self-respect before the umlaut. In fact, if he had made any proper contact at all, the rest of the manoeuvre would have looked after itself. But for some reason not apparent from my point of vantage, Dorf chose this moment to deflect the gonad backwards into the path of Nriwi, whose alacrity had been a feature of proceedings, and who arkled without slowing from a curving run that finished in front of the main stand with the delighted crowd rising in its place and calling his name. Dorf claimed later that he had failed to allow for the wind. When told that the wind was recorded at zero, Dorf said that he had possibly failed to allow sufficiently for a lack of wind.

The young Zambians lack cohesion, but their arkeling has a wonderful spontaneous quality, and there can be little doubt that Tuesday's final score flattered the victors. Nriwi, particularly, is a player of whom we shall hear more.

This was not the first close shave for Australia in recent days. The Cubans came within a blither of a famous victory in Perth the previous Thursday. Had Sorenson not been moved into the centre in the final minutes, and had he not imposed his authority on the fixture by peeling off three arkles of surpassing subtlety (one of them while lying down as his thigh was being strapped by a handler) and had he not neutralised the hitherto devastating Tostaro, the result would undoubtedly have favoured the visitors.

Of the leaden performance against Scotland on 27 October, enough has probably already been written. It is easy to find fault with the players, and certainly on the grommit, where it counts, mistakes have been made. Of course they have. No one would deny it. Wylie's lateral traverse against the Cubans opened up the entire left-hand end of the splicing-zone. Dorf's almost complete loss of confidence in his team mates and the team's nearly total loss of confidence in Dorf are possibly driving a wedge between Dorf and the rest of the side.

Things are not good and the players will need to find something if their world ranking is to be retained. But it can't all be put at the door of the players. The decision by the World Farnarkeling body to ban Australia from further competition after the next World Championships has had a very debilitating effect. Players who used to train for hours with smiles on their faces now sit and look out the window. The talk is of retirement and of the past. The Australian Government's attitude to Aboriginal policy is well known, and it is difficult to see any softening of their position.

The South Africans have proposed a tour and have outlined a programme of encounters between the two nations beginning in January and running through until somewhere in the second half of April, but with the exception of Dorf, the players have declined the offer. Sorenson is said to have been offered $250,000 to take an unofficial invitation team called The Official Australian Farnarkeling Team and appear in selected cities for three weeks. Three weeks is known to be a bad time for Sorenson, and he is not expected to accept. The standard of play by the national representatives has fallen off by all means, but it is a difficult and very disappointing period for them.

What they need at the moment is support and encouragement and what they do not need is Cyril Dorf writing to the newspaper with his unusual interpretation of international politics. Cyril Dorf, it should be remembered, led the movement against the introduction of the $53^{1}/_{2}$ metre penalty line because, he said, it punished initiative and favoured players with frizzy hair. He also appeared on "Have Your Say" and argued the point with Evan Harrua and Grgtrt Ydklrg. The spectacle of members of the Federal Executive sniping at each other on national television was a lasting embarrassment to the code and not one to be repeated. Cyril has a son in the Australian Squad and a daughter in Telecom and should be well pleased. He must consider the consequences of his actions, however, and those members of the press who seek to fan the fires should study their history. The last time Cyril Dorf turned up at an after-match function an incident occurred which reflected badly on the character of the louvre windows and obliged Sorenson to miss the game against Honduras.

Challenge Round Wide
Open at this Stage

Tuesday night.

Ideal conditions prevailed in Perth late yesterday for the staging of the first two fixtures in the regional section of the challenge round build-up for the World Championships currently expected to be decided in either Rangoon or Amsterdam in early August, Australian time.

In a fast-moving and very enjoyable curtain raiser, the gallant Nepalese went down to the more experienced Canadians, but not before giving the Great White Northerners a little something to be going on with. Lacking the height or the reach of their opposition, the Nepalese Brains Trust had worked out a series of well-prepared running moves, particularly through the centre and down the right-hand flange, playing mainly to Nanyad, the deceptively fast utility back whose dominance of McSixpack will surely have the Mounties in the back-room grouped in a circle.

The second encounter was delayed for 45 minutes when it was discovered that the clock was running 45 minutes fast and that to start on time would therefore be to begin 45 minutes early. The committee decided that rather than start on time and be 45 minutes early, they would start 45 minutes late and be on time. As a result, the radio broadcast of the main fixture was replaced by an announcement that because play had already finished, the live commentary would be transmitted as soon as it hadn't started yet. There followed some light music and a list of river heights.

In the event, Australia came from behind to edge out a determined Poland in an evenly contested and free-flowing affair from which the home side can take some satisfaction but from which it must also learn. The Poles, notably Katjscinski, Wotjekzniski and the evergreen Witold Osip were very strong in the flanks and around the whiffenwacker, and their consistent ability to run the gonad out of defence and take the Australians by surprise meant that both Stavridos and Wylie had to be moved into the plonking box, and the Australian frontal attack was left in the unlikely hands of Neville Dorf and Stewie Davidson. Dorf's inclusion in the side had been openly questioned by many experts, including most of the capacity crowd. (The publication of his book, *The Genius of Neville Dorf*, after only two appearances for his country, had led to suggestions that his commitment to the team was perhaps less than absolute, and his only significant performance had been against the Madagascans when Australia had an insuperable lead and Dorf arkled by accident while attempting to hit the opposing captain in the ovipositor while the referee was unavoidably detained underneath a pile of other contestants.)

He and Stewie Davidson posed no threat to the Poles. Davidson seems to have lost a metre or two of his pace and by the look of his fuselage he had a particularly enjoyable Christmas.

As expected, the focus of the match was the tussle between the dangerously fit Wojek Conrad and the very remarkable Dave Sorenson. Conrad had got away from Sorenson several times early in the second warble and seemed poised to take command, but Sorenson, who had been on antibiotics to clear up a blockage in the Eustachian tubes that had caused him to surprise himself while sneezing, proceeded to take the initiative and turn on a display of arkeling that will linger in the memory. The crowning achievement was probably the Inverse Blither he performed while running backwards by reversing the position of his feet and by leaping both up and sideways as the gonad was intercepted and despatched at apparently different altitudes simultaneously. The wall he hit will be shifted before the second round of matches beginning on the 24th.

Standings after Saturday: Group 1: China 1, Burma 1, Peru 1, Singapore 1, Norway 1, Angola 1, Tanzania 1, Canada 1, Zambia 1, Australia 1, Corfu 1, Hungary 1, German Democratic Republic 1, Italy 0, France 0, Nepal 0, South Korea 0, Sudan 0, Algeria 0, Poland 0, Uruguay 0, Vanuatu 0, Laos 0, England 0, Portugal 0, Ross Dependencies 0. (Mexico had a bye.)

The Run Home

Australian farnarkeling received a much needed shot in the arm with the news that Australia has eliminated Sweden in a nip-and-tuck affair in sub-zero temperatures at the all-weather Farnarkeling Centre in Gottenburg earlier today, Australian time.

Dave Sorenson, the Parvo Nurmi of Australian Farnarkeling, was prominent throughout and set Australia up with a powerhouse display in an explosive third warble. The axiomatic Sorenson, who was cleared to play only moments before the phlange was lowered, was all over the opposition until a spring went in his knee and he lost all feeling in the hormones. Sorenson is now in doubt for the semifinal against either Scotland or Taiwan and it will be tragic indeed if they can't unscrew him before the weekend.

Australians into Final

Farnarkeling history was made last night in Madrid when Australia confounded the experts and bundled Scotland out of an incident-packed semifinal in front of an estimated crowd.

In near-perfect conditions on a beautifully prepared grommet the Australians began well and wore the plucky Caledonians down with a combination of accurate lunging and superior fitness. Once again the very dextrous Dave Sorenson dominated the attacking phase and, after a short time, was arkeling from all points of the compass. Unfortunately, he suffered a spectacular mishap in the middle of the fourth warble when he dislodged a pinion in the goalpost-housing and impaled himself on the Southern Wall. It'll be tragic indeed if he can't be prised off the facilities in time to take his place in the side for what promises to be the final against the East Germans in Moscow next weekend.

Historic Victory

The Australian farnarkelers were literally on top of the world last night following their epoch-making victory against the formidable East German farnarkeling machine in a closely-contested final at the People's Farnarkeling Centre in light drizzle and heavy security in Moscow.

The ruthlessly professional East Germans began strongly and had the Australians reeling from a series of quite obvious and very brutal personal fouls. But just after the leiderkrantz it became obvious that the continually impressive Dave Sorenson had weathered the bone-crushing first warble and was prepared to take the fixture right up to the East Germans after the umlaut. The turning-point came in the third warble when the oleagenous Sorenson arkeled from behind his own goal-line despite being held by both opposing fullbacks and a small ice-flattening machine he'd inadvertently backed into during a lapse in concentration. Unfortunately, only moments later, he struck an overhead light with a wet knee and short circuited his trousers. It'll be tragic indeed if he can't be de-ionised in time to return home to what promises to be a hero's welcome in Sydney on Tuesday night.

Conquering Heroes Return

The victorious Australian farnarkeling team returned home in triumph last night with the bevelled orb safe in their keeping until the challenge round in late July, Australian time.

Team members were fulsome in their praise of the running of the championships and are approaching the government to get an arkeling grommet of international standard built in Canberra so overseas teams can provide much needed competition here during the Northern summer.

The heavily-bandaged Dave Sorenson, who aggravated a thigh injury with a heavy fall from the aircraft while deplaning before the ramp was in position, reacted strongly to suggestions that corporate sponsorship is poised to take farnarkeling into commercial television.

Proposals are already with the governing body to introduce a solid programme of one-day farnarkeling fixtures under lights with edited highlights between the warbles and a viewer competition tentatively called "Classic Arkels". Major manufacturers have already come up with what they claim is the definitive farnarkeling shoe, and t-shirts and initiatives in fast food are already in the pipeline.

The well-credentialled Sorenson said he would have nothing whatever to do with what he described as "A ridiculous farnarkeling circus" which he claimed would turn the game into some kind of joke. Although he did admit he had been approached.

It will be very unfortunate for arkelophiles if Sorenson's assault hearing coincides with the exhibition match in Perth next Friday.

A capacity crowd was treated to a display of champagne farnarkeling in an exhibition fixture run in Perth on Friday to aid world famine relief.

In an all-star engagement the victorious Australian world championship side lined up against a composite invitation team from other farnarkeling countries. The national side quickly demonstrated its total mastery of the code and pulled out every type of arkel from all parts of the grommet and seemed to have the flukem on a string, particularly when moving forward in defence. The very dextrous Dave Sorenson, who seems to set new standards every time he steps onto the sward, was in inspirational form and the game has never had a better ambassador. He was instrumental in one almost magical arkel just before the umlaut when he notched one up from well outside the whiffenwacker by deflecting the gonad with his foot while being tackled. He was later involved in an unfortunate altercation with a section of wire netting at the southern end of the concourse and it'll be tragic indeed if he can't be disengaged in time for the Sportsman of the Year Dinner, where he is the red- hot favourite to pick up the big one.

Sorenson Honoured

Dave Sorenson was named Sportsman of the Year at a well-attended post-prandial black-tie wallop in Sydney earlier this evening, Australian time.

The heavily-bandaged but very dignified Sorenson, the Mick Young of Australian farnarkeling, was given a standing ovation as an edited sequence of some of his more spectacular arkels was projected on to a makeshift grommet positioned in the ceiling at the back of the transom-housing.

Unfortunately, Sorenson suffered a catastrophic personal mishap while mounting the podium to pick up the sculpted tribute. He hadn't looked well since the soup and it was no surprise to onlookers when he fell through a rostrum interstice only seconds later while raising the golden artefact and thanking his immediate family.

Organisers said that this was the first time since the function's inception that the award had been taken internally and it'll be tragic indeed if the accoladectomy can't be performed in time for Sorenson to attend the launch of the Farnarkeling Federation's new televised drive for popular support.

Newspaper & Radio

1985-1989

*In the mid 1980s Mr Dagg began contributing
to various newspapers and also returned to radio,
addressing matters of the utmost importance, usually with
common sense and a piece of baling-twine.*

Spot the Deliberate Mistake

In response to questions from confused members of the Australian public, many of whom are known to me personally, I've embarked on a programme of national education.

Too little is written about the ignorance of the Australian people. There is, by way of contrast, too much written about their intelligence. Their resourcefulness, initiative and fearless traditions have been set to music in order to sell a wide range of foreign products; the Anzac spirit is evoked by no one more beautifully than American fast food chains, and the chairman of Australian Steel has been made a Sacred Treasure by the government of Japan.

The problem of educating the Australian population is clearly urgent and must be addressed on a scale never before contemplated. We've started at a very rudimentary level with a massive television campaign designed to teach people what a Post Office is. We've tried to do several things at once, which is a sophisticated concept, but one we like. We're explaining:

(a) What a Post Office is.

(b) Who those people are, in Post Office uniforms, who deliver your mail.

(c) What those things are, that are put in your letter box (through a slot in many cases) by the uniformed artisans mentioned in (b).

(d) What those boxes are. (The ones in which articles are placed by the liveried representatives of the essential service industry alluded to in (a).)

(e) That when it's raining, the mail is delivered in the rain.

(f) That during periods of intense sunshine, the mail is not delivered in the rain.

(g) That, in order to effect delivery, some postal employees use bicycles, although on very steep hills, particularly when the mail is not being delivered in the rain, the bicycle may choose not to be ridden but to be pushed.

We've referred to the Post Office throughout as 'Australia Post', a catchy name meaning Post Office. In fact, we've been even cleverer than this would imply. We've decided to improve our logo. Initially, I wasn't sure this was possible. The old logo has been extremely successful and, despite claims that it was unnecessary and meaningless, research has demonstrated that many people realised eventually that the logo had something to do with Australia Post, which, of course, they associated with the Post Office. Aside from these practical considerations, the logo is very appealing to the eye and is a fine example of Australian design at its triumphant best.

There is no limit to the amount of money we're prepared to spend on developing a new logo. The cost is simply not a factor. The stakes are too high for petty mercantile considerations to be of any significance. What we'd like to do is annihilate our competition so comprehensively that it will be almost as if it hadn't existed.

I know this all sounds new, but we've done something very like it before. We ran a visually very satisfying campaign some time ago explaining to people what a telephone is. (In effect, a telephone is a thing that rings in the mountains of southern Europe, and the ringing stops if you pick it up and cry into it.) It worked better than we dared hope and, at the time of writing, there is now only one organisation operating nationally as a provider of telephone services.

In some countries, of course, both Telecom and the Post Office would be owned by the state, and the millions spent on advertising would be wasted on improving services and lowering costs.

So buoyant did we feel after all of the above, and such was the feeling around the office, that we decided to keep going. Gamblers will know what I mean when I say we felt we were 'on a roll'. It was resolved on a show of hands that we adopt the suggestion made by the young work-experience person, and change the name of TAA. We tinkered briefly with the conceptual work and decided to call it either 'Australian Airlines' or 'Australia Post'. We eliminated 'Telecom' because we wanted to avoid imagery of mountains and crying and making expensive telephone calls to women who live alone in Surrey. After a heated lunch we also ruled out 'Australia Post' because, despite the many common elements (uniforms, rain and sunshine), aeroplane travel and group cycling are fundamentally different. We felt this difference demanded expression. Very few of the sample group associated the name 'Australian Airlines' with the Post Office, and TAA is, as everybody has known for years, an Australian airline. Simple really: 'Australian Airlines'.

But how to sell it, how to market this intricate and yet muscular idea? The answer was, of course again, educate the people. Paint all the aircraft, order new badges, new paper, new hats, new buildings, new front doors for the vans (the cost of all this to be charged against 'Improvements'). Follow this with a massive multi-media campaign, trumpeting the arrival of a completely new airline that no one has ever heard of, and which only a small number of people will think of as the Post Office. I have seen criticism of our decisions, but it is petty and ill-informed. I will not dignify it with a response.

Helpful Suggestions

I don't mean to harp on about this, but there still isn't anything like enough public money being syphoned into the advertising industry. There are plenty of government-owned bodies spending virtually nothing on nebulous ideas and anthem quality statements of the obvious.

I exclude the Post Office from this. I know I've been critical of them in the past, but my hat is now raised in a gesture of respect. Their television commercials have made them the market leader right across the country.

They have filletted the competition to the point where, I believe I am right in saying, in some areas the Post Office is now the only Post Office still operating as a Post Office.

I also have only the highest regard for the millions sensibly invested by Telecom in establishing that a telephone can be used for making phone calls. I may have oversimplified this. The commercials actually indicate that a telephone can be used for making overseas or interstate phone calls. There is no suggestion that it is possible to make local calls, but there is probably a reason for this. Perhaps the phone is out of order and no one can look at it before Wednesday, or maybe all the phones in the whole area are out and nobody knows why, or it is possible that the phone has been cut off because the user is too poor to go on helping with the TV commercials.

Neither do I intend any disrespect to the airline that used to be TAA. Their work in establishing whatever their new name is has been without parallel in the history of image-based money flushing, although they didn't have it all their own way. The Buy Australia Campaign must have given them an awful fright.

This was a bench-mark effort. It pointed out that people should not buy Australian products just because they were Australian. This broke down the old, stereotyped idea that a commercial should achieve what it set out to do. The Buy Australia Campaign depended for its success on the ability of the buying public to reject the advice of its advertising. I'm presuming here that the aim of the campaign was to encourage people to buy Australian products, supposing such a thing were possible.

It would be unfair to ignore also the spectacular media spending embarked upon in the name of the Priority One Campaign. It would not be at all appropriate to remember the campaign itself, but the figures involved were very reassuring.

For the Bicentennial one can have only the most open-hearted admiration. Not only are they currently funding about a quarter of the world's shipping, but the plan to sail the *Deficit* around Australia during the summer months is well advanced and the television campaign is on air, even though it obviously isn't quite finished yet. There is a song about all of us doing something without hands. I'm sure it will all become clear once it has been edited.

It is what is called an 'awareness' campaign. It doesn't sell anything or provide any actual information. Its main aim is to be on television. It can then be demonstrated that a number of people might have watched it. They will be 'aware' of it.

Whether or not the Bicentennial can recover from this advantage remains to be seen. There can be little doubt, however, that so far they are doing everything expected of them.

What I want to know is, where are the other government departments? Where are the awareness campaigns for the Weather Bureau and the Official Receiver? Should their Australian-ness not be celebrated?

Would not the romance of Soil Erosion lend itself to the screen? It is Australian Soil Erosion, after all. It is the best bloody Soil Erosion in the world and it wants to tell its story. A more natural subject for a song would be difficult to imagine. It has everything; wind, rain, floods, the pitiless heat of the sun. Perhaps the Weather Bureau could be part of it. The Official Receiver should also be approached without delay.

There are others, of course. The Albury-Wodonga Development Corporation, for instance. Isn't this the sort of dream that sustained the lads in trenches all over France and Belgium? Is there an Australian heart that does not quicken at the mention of The Inspector of Inflammable Liquids or the Department of Lifts and Cranes?

These people cannot be expected to continue unless their work is accorded the simple dignity of being described within an inch of its life and sung about by groups of white Australians who are not hanging from prison ceilings.

A Bold Future for Broadcasting

There seems to be some opposition to this business of amalgamating the ABC and SBS. Good grief. Let me explain.

We have been wondering what to do with the ABC. We've had various studies done, and a series of commissions have been established over the years to look into the performance of one another, and it has all come to a head recently because of a need to rationalise the operation in line with current policy.

The short list of suggestions at the planning meeting was predictably impressive.

1. Change the name of the ABC to Australian Airlines and run a series of commercials, costing whatever, depicting a large group of uniformed employees becoming very excited about being filmed being very excited. Possibly with a rousing airpunching anthem and plenty of booming drums.

2. Change its name to Australia Post and run a lot of expensive commercials showing the capacity for things to be done during weather.

3. Amalgamate the ABC with Telecom and commission a string of increasingly perceptive commercials establishing that millions of dollars worth of glossy advertising will make management feel better. (This has yet to be established, but I'm pretty sure something of the sort must be the case.)

4. Designate the ABC as the official mouthpiece of the Buy Australian campaign. Advantage: we wouldn't have to give a great deal of public money away to a small group who control the communications industry. Disadvantage: we wouldn't be able to give a great deal of public money away to a small group who control the communications industry.

5. Sell the ABC to the highest bidder, bearing in mind that there are no bidders. The ABC has only one thing worth buying: its audience. The question is not how to privatise the ABC, where the news now consists almost entirely of promotions for stories yet to come, and well-woven thank-yous between news people and sports people and weather people, and frequent announcements by reporters of their names and where they are and sometimes even the date and the fact that they are appearing on ABC news, which is not as surprising to the audience as you might expect. There is obviously little time left for news, and it's hardly surprising there isn't any. They've also employed someone to talk over the credits of the programmes in a voice that makes three syllables of "and" the way

they do on commercial television, which many people don't like, which is why the ABC's audience exists.

A substantial part of this audience has already gone to SBS, certainly for news and current affairs and such things as entertainment. If we amalgamate them while simultaneously destroying the ABC's already reduced capacity to deliver to what remains of its own audience, we'll force the audience either to commercial television or away from television altogether, thereby privatising that audience.

There remains ABC Radio, which is the best known example of the relationship between the smell of an oily rag and the will to keep going. They hide in the hills, these people, and they come down at night, destroying railway lines and making off with army property. We know who they are. We have names.

We remain, of course, deeply committed to the maintenance of the very highest standards in broadcasting in Australia, and we salute ABC management in this regard.

The Romance of Banking

I don't want to seem to be over-reacting here, but there have been a number of unfortunate remarks made about the very sensible decision by some of the people in the banking dodge to institute charges for cheques. Personally I can't see that it's anyone else's business what banks charge their customers, in fact I'm surprised that they have gone to the trouble of telling their customers the new arrangements are about to be introduced.

The charges are completely justified and more or less essential. Banks provide services to their customers, and some of the customers – not all, but some of them – have been abusing the system by using the services. They open a cheque account, for instance, and then sit down and write a whole lot of cheques.

Now this sort of thing is not on. A cheque account is supposed to be a convenience, by all means, but not for the customer. Let's look at the facts. A cheque account is opened and a range of charges come into effect straight away, the meter is running from the kickoff, and no matter how much money is in the account, the bank never pays any interest unless the customer puts the money in a different account, where it can't be got at so easily, and if the account is overdrawn the bank charges interest as well as the charges and it charges charges to charge the interest, which is only fair.

They don't always trouble the customer with a formal announcement of this, they just do a little takeaway sum down the right-hand side and put the money in another account marked 'whoopee'.

If money is deposited from another account held by the customer, the interest-bearing total in that account decreases, obviously, and the bank charges a fee for transferring the money, which again is fair enough when you consider the amount of work involved. On top of which, of course, the bank then safeguards the customer's money. Particularly, as it happens, from the customer. If the customer goes into the local bank where the staff consists almost entirely of members of the customer's immediate family, small amounts of money can be obtained by standing in a queue among video machines depicting holidays in places the customer can't afford to go.

If the customer turns up at another branch of the bank and writes a cheque, the bank safeguards the customer's money by assuming that the customer is someone else who has stolen the customer's chequebook and the customer's accreditation from the bank, identification, driver's licence and credit cards, and frequently some of the customer's children, and is on some kind of rampage with the customer's very limited funding.

Of course, if someone comes in with some money, and looks like an identikit photograph and wants the money deposited in 15 different names and, if there are any problems, ring this number and ask for the tooth fairy, that's obviously OK.

Perhaps the romance of banking does not weave its happy spell over every heart, and I fully understand that my own case may be unusual.

I ran away from home at the age of nine in order to go into merchant banking and I was fortunate enough to secure a position as a deckhand with one of the bigger operators. As the name might imply, my job was mainly in the service and backup area. If people didn't pay on time, I used to deck them with my hand.

In time, of course, I went into international money management. I was given an eye-patch and a parrot and was told to put in for water some time near the end of June.

I don't intend to chronicle my entire career here, but banking has a human side and I often find that a personal anecdote can break down a prejudice and open the mind of a bigoted person.

People must understand that the plight of Australian banks at the moment is one which concerns us all. I won't go into too much chapter and verse on the history of this because, frankly, we still don't know quite how it happened, but somehow the banks have found themselves providing a service to their customers. The position could not be more serious.

The problem is a thing called Bankcard. We introduced it a few years ago in order to encourage people to get into debt so we could charge them interest on money we knew they didn't have.

We nominated a date by which the money we knew they didn't have had to be paid back and, when it wasn't, we reluctantly hopped into them for the going rate.

We advertised it as a convenience, which of course it was, since we were able to do all this without even leaving the building. The retailers took to the idea immediately.

The old convention of selling goods only to those who can afford to pay for them had long hampered the retail trade, but now they could sell to anyone and they began laying in stocks of anything at all in a full range of colours.

The right to insult the customer was retained by the practice of checking each Bankcard against a secret list of axe-murderers provided by Interpol and kept somewhere under the counter.

It was all going fairly well and bankers all over the country were fighting to keep a straight face when suddenly the appalling truth became apparent. Many individuals were actually paying their Bankcard accounts when they received them. People were, in effect, paying the card off as they used it.

In other words, the only return to the bank was from all the customers' other accounts, from loans, mortgages, leasing arrangements, property speculation, overdrafts, service fees, duties, levies, general adjustments and whatever alterations to interest rates seemed like a good idea at the time.

Compensation and restitution must be paid to banks immediately if the economy is to remain upright. Freeloading and other forms of deception must stop. The public has selfishly and wilfully abused a very noble experiment and the proposed $30 charge for Bankcard will not go close to covering the damage.

The following initiatives must be introduced if the banking industry is to survive.

• A $40 fee charged to people who don't have a Bankcard. This is only fair.

• A handling fee of $5 on all transactions of any type at any bank during banking hours.

• Bank officials to be authorised to wear balaclavas and to cosh likely prospects in the street at a rate not exceeding 150 an hour.

• The reintroduction of deckhands.

It is only through improvements of this kind that Australian society's present values can be maintained.

An Independent View

There is a great deal of publicity being given at the moment to an outfit called the New Right. This is because the Old Right (who tend to own such trinkets as radio and television stations, magazines, newspapers and other items covered by the Not Nailed Down legislation) have decided to stimulate debate in order to keep the government on its toes while the trapdoor is oiled and the shadow cabinet is fitted into a landing craft.

I was a foundation member of the New Right and have been involved in the development of much of the New Right philosophy. I reluctantly left the movement in late August following an internal wrangle over the colour of the tunic and the insignia on the hat. However disappointed I might have been by what was, for me, a watering down of our original aims, I nevertheless still share many of the ideas and aspirations I see being broadcast through our official outlets.

That said, I note with mounting concern an apparently wilful failure in some quarters to fully understand what we are saying. I blame education for this, and I'll tell you something for nothing; when we get in again, the loonies in the teacher unions will hit the ground running. I heard a schoolteacher the other day on a radio programme about children (for Christ's sake) saying that every school anywhere in Australia should be able to provide a good standard of education. To which my response is "No thank you very much, indeed. Begging your pardon, but we don't live in Russia. Not yet!" I digress, I'm sorry, but education was one of my areas of responsibility, and I won't abide cant.

In essence, the philosophies of the New Right are based on a recognition of the value of the individual and an abhorrence of anything that stands in the way of the individual, such as unions, bureaucracies, taxation, regulation or other individuals.

I can perhaps best illustrate this by example. We favour the introduction of university fees, although I forget why, because obviously only the wealthier type of individual will be in attendance. We oppose land rights on some very sound basis that just eludes me for the moment, and we favour uranium exports to France because of a wide range of factors. We favour the idea of people working for the dole because it provides a sense of dignity for the people for whom the people on the dole are working, and it gives the unemployed an opportunity to work without contributing to anything approaching a wages explosion. There is absolutely no need for a Commission for the Future because we favour uranium exports to France, and we question the alleged 'right' of single mothers to benefits from the state. If we start giving way to one group, pretty soon we'll have the taxpayers' money being used to help bloody near anyone who needs help! This defeats the very purpose of taxation, which is to find ways of reducing taxation.

I might say, while I've got you all here, that these views are not simply those of a small group outside the mainstream of Australian politics. The Liberal Party contains many of our leading lights, the Labor Government is implementing some of our more imaginative suggestions and, although I appreciate that many people find it necessary to deplore us loudly at dinner parties, I think we are all sufficiently grown up to know what's really going on, and I hope as many of you as possible can make it to the barbecue on the 15th.

Hands Across the Tasman

My first contact with Australians was in London, where I was living during the early 1970s for tax purposes. At one stage, seeking a career in retailing, I wrapped mail orders in the back of the book department of Harrods. Each volume was placed on a piece of corrugated cardboard and the cardboard was then manipulated until the book was no longer visible. A skill I have never lost.

Across the bench from me was an Australian who called everyone Bruce. He pointed out a friend of his in the sports department. "See him, Bruce?" he said. "He's a professional tennis player."

"What's he doing working in the sports department of Harrods if he's a professional tennis player?" I asked.

"He's no good," said the Australian.

I lasted three days at Harrods, but my Australian friend lacked my persistence and was impeached on the second afternoon for putting a famous sign on the main stairs. It was made of corrugated cardboard and said: HARRODS, NO FARTING.

It was at this point that I recognised the shared perspective of Australia and New Zealand on matters of international significance. The question is whether or not this communion of subversives can be converted into export dollars.

Closer Economic Relations will do much for the exchange of ideas among business people, of course, although it should be remembered that there is really only one idea among business people and exchanging it is an achievement of only modest dimensions. It must surely be possible to develop something more worthwhile than the intercourse of moustachioed primates in Flag Inns all over both countries.

A new nation should obviously be forged, combining the two in such a way as to maximise the contribution of each. Australia would grow fine wools, beef and trees for Rupert's newspapers. New Zealand can provide dairy products, coarse wools and trees for Rupert's other newspapers. Representatives from both countries should be elected to a new government, possibly in Brisbane, where there hasn't been one for a while and where it will have novelty value.

Roger Douglas is an automatic selection as Minister for Finance. Someone would have to explain the job to him, but once he understood it he'd be hard to hold. He is dedicated to excellence in all things and is apparently a delightful person. His appointment would also eliminate the need for the portfolios of Health, Education, Social Welfare, Housing, Agriculture and the Arts.

Advice should also be provided from the Australian Treasury. This remarkable body has only the democratic process standing between it and world domination. Under the sacred banners of building the savings pool and reducing external debt, it has guided a succession of governments to the sunlit upland of internal debt and the ennobling of financial institutions and serious fund managers. The man who runs Standard and Poor's Australian office, who increased Australia's credit rating and spoke favourably of the sound management of the economy reflected in the federal budget, worked previously for the Australian Treasury, writing the federal budget. This is clearly not an outfit to be ignored, and my suggestion is that we get to them early and ask what it would cost to have them aboard.

Winston Peters would be Speaker. He has been trying to curb this tendency lately but there seems little point and a man who only shaves because it provides him with an audience has much to offer an emerging nation. If the post of Governor-General is available, I would suggest almost anyone except Greg Chappell and Richard Loe, and I submit the following changes to the governmental structure of all states in the new federation.

The bicameral system obliges the government of the day to deal with vestiges of the last government but three. The same thing happens when cousins marry, and quite clearly there should be one House, as is the case in New Zealand, with the proviso that the power should be retained by the states, as is the case in Australia. This will allow for spirited debate and important pronouncements which have nothing to do with the running of the country, and will accommodate both the New Zealand yearning for regional independence and the Australian desire for a perpetual constitutional crisis.

The new Parliamentary buildings in Canberra and Wellington can then be turned into all-weather sporting complexes, thereby satisfying the only genuine interest of the entire population of both countries.

The Resolution of Conflict

In which a mature understanding is brought to certain delicate questions and from which it may be deduced that a fat lot of good it is, too.

Industrial Unrest Crisis Point

An uneasy truce, in existence since members of the Federated Under Tens' Association accepted a package of long-term benefits and returned to work a month ago, is showing signs of fraying at the edges.

The Massed Five-Year-Olds have grown in strength, having changed jobs this year, forgoing a part-time casual consultancy pasting pieces of refuse together and reassuring one another as to the circular persistence of the wheels on the bus, in favour of a full-time tenured position painting themselves green and hanging upside down from garden furniture.

The curfew introduced in early February, as part of a range of initiatives designed to improve operational standards following the annual break, has not been accepted at all well. The Federated Under Tens were known to be opposed to curfews, and a rather inept and politically dangerous attempt was made by management to introduce one without calling it a curfew.

The FUT read the mood of the meeting beautifully, and boldly decided that the correct response to something that was pretending not to be a curfew was to pretend to accept it. This prevented the problem from emerging as a theoretical discussion and consequently a number of hours are now being lost through regular tests of muscle and endurance on the evening shift.

The moment the curfew is in effect, the trouble begins. Within minutes, as if by prearranged signal, one of the delegates is located in a restricted area. Offenders are frequently apprehended carrying contraband goods, impounded literature or rolls of Sellotape, which they are believed to be storing somewhere, possibly in an underground warehouse.

On one recent occasion, a delegate was found holding down the flushing mechanism on a toilet in order to simulate ablutionary activity, while another delegate was pushing a member of the Australian Association of Dogs around in a cardboard box. When asked to explain the merits of this exercise, one of the delegates described their purpose as being in some way related to dental hygiene. The AAD made no official comment, but its representative was clearly embarrassed and will perhaps not be so easily coerced again.

This followed a heated exchange in mid-February when authorities investigating unusual sounds were surprised to walk in on a trampolining contest in what was listed as a dormitory zone. This had obviously been in progress for some time as those involved were perspiring freely and the area had sustained serious structural damage.

Government stepped in. The position was said by government to be one of the utmost gravity. Safety standards were being jeopardised, product quality was down. Such privileges as had previously been negotiated would be subject to immediate review, said government, if this sort of thing did not stop forthwith.

The following night an office-bearer in the Massed Fives was found to be conducting a series of commando-style raids on the food refrigeration facility. The facts were difficult to obtain in this instance because the accused was wearing a stackhat and could not hear the carefully worded questions of security personnel.

Other outstanding disputes include the long-running controversy about the clothing allowance, which is said by the FUT to be completely inadequate and which ministry representatives have described as "very generous indeed".

Regulations currently in force lay down parameters for the cleansing, refurbishing and replacement of suitable clothing to reasonable levels. It is this last phrase upon which the disagreement pivots. For example, regulations express a need for two socks per person per day, such to be returned. The FUT wants "unless lost" to be added to this requirement, and it wants the number increased from two to 27.

The Massed Fives are pushing for alternative legislation providing for a particular set of clothes, deemed ideal for prevailing conditions, to be cleaned daily and not varied by management without the express written consent of the wearer; any variation or other breach of this understanding to be met with instant withdrawal of all services by the Massed Fives, and any attempt at arbitration to be rejected well above acceptable noise levels.

The overall position is considered by experts to be about as average as anyone can remember. No one can remember a time when the overall position was less perfectly normal than it is now. All parties are said to be hopeful of an early settlement and are planning to meet first thing in the morning provided they get enough sleep.

Entire Country Held to Ransom

Australia ground to a virtual halt on Tuesday when the Federated Under Tens' Association withdrew services, stating that in their view it was an unreasonable demand that they wear a sunhat in the sun. They further suggested that the placement of sunscreen lotion on or about their persons was an infringement of basic human rights and was "simply not on".

A compromise was reached when it was conceded that they should not come over here and do it, but that someone would go over there and do it, and that, yes, they could go to Timmy and Simone's afterwards.

Wednesday saw the dispute widen when an affiliated body, the Massed Five-Year-Olds, showed their hand by waiting until the temperature had built up and management had about 50 kilograms of essential foodstuffs in transit from supermarket to transport and then sitting down on the footpath over a log of claims relating to ice cream.

The Federated Under Tens, sensing blood in the water, immediately lodged a similar demand and supported the Massed Five-Year-Olds by pretending to have a breakdown as a result of cruelty and appalling conditions.

The problem had been further exacerbated by a breakage to one of the food-carrying receptacles and some consequent structural damage to several glass bottles and a quantity of eggs, the contents of which were beginning to impinge on the well-being of the public thoroughfare.

Government stepped in. Government expressed itself in the form of a brief address. Ice cream would be provided, explained an official, but not simply because it has been demanded. This was not the way to achieve results and no repetition of this sort of thing would be tolerated.

A highly-ranked source in the Under Tens said: "We regret that we have to take this type of action. Believe me, we tried reason."

"Strawberry," said someone from the Massed Fives, "with pineapple and blue heaven."

Relations seemed to have stabilised by Thursday, following substantial reorganisation along the lines of a collectivist approach to decision-making. The Federated Under Tens and the Massed Fives were awake to the possibilities here and, by block-voting and the use of secret hand signals, they dominated meetings and might have taken complete control of policy formation had it not been for an unfortunate incident in which an office-bearer in the FUT was arrested for the attempted murder of the National Secretary of the MFYO in an internal disagreement about Textacolour ownership.

An attempt to establish clearly marked territories and separate job definitions was unsuccessful as it was the preferred option of each group that it should have the territory and the other should have the jobs. The matter was deadlocked at tea and a cooling-down period was necessary before negotiations could continue.

The evening was passed quietly except for a near tragedy when the local representative of the Australian Association of Dogs upset the fragile ceasefire by sitting on the Ludo while nobody was looking.

Friday was a lay-day as the site was visited by independent authorities from the National Union of Grandparents, a benevolent organisation thought to be funded by the Tea Industry.

Differences were forgotten and any slight flare-ups were resolved by the laying-on of hands or, in one rather more passionate instance, by the laying-on of feet.

By mid-morning on Saturday, interest rates were improving and both major industrial groups seemed happy with production levels and working conditions. At 1100 hours sunhats were provided and a protective lotion was distributed to all personnel. At first there seemed to be no objection. Then the FUT refused point-blank to put them on or to handle them in any way and the MFYO, in flagrant contravention of previous undertakings, demanded ice cream and plenty of it.

Prospects for the rest of the year look a little bleak from here. I can only wish you well.

Winter of Discontent

There is a feeling in the market that during recent months the unions have quite consciously prevented disputes from flaring up in a random and isolated fashion, and have instead been stockpiling ammunition for a comprehensive showdown. It promises to be a top-of-the-range affair and tickets should be booked early.

There are several very major problems. The Federated Under Tens have had a range of grievances festering since early in the June quarter, when new clothing regulations were introduced. The Under Tens were known to be against regulations of any sort and their reaction to the provision of compulsory wet-weather gear was predictably hostile, despite the fact that the principal reason for the introduction of wet-weather gear was the wetness of the weather.

All personnel were issued with the standard kit consisting of 1 x raincoat, 1 x warm hat, 1 x pair of gumboots and 1 x pair of warm socks.

The Federated Under Tens saw this as a calculated attempt to subject them to ridicule and further worsen their standing in the community. The Massed Fives were frankly insulted by the whole business. Stripped of its fancy language, they said, it meant that their members would be asked to accept substandard garments that had been discarded by members of the FUT. Such garments were quite obviously second-hand, very old, extremely unattractive and, according to a highly placed source in the Massed Fives, this was "typical". It was suggested that management was favouring the Federated Under Tens by attempting to co-opt them into a sweetheart deal with promises of new clothing.

Management denied this ludicrous charge and initiated discussions with the Massed Fives to see whether or not they could be attracted into a sweetheart deal of their own relating to some new socks. This rather messy and ill-advised approach backfired immediately. The Massed Fives made it clear that any settlement would have to include a new hat, a new coat (of a type specified by delegates according to taste), a proper pair of boots and, ideally, a book about dinosaurs.

Independent tests were conducted by the National Union of Grandparents, a charitable order made up of ex-management personnel who had a pretty easy ride while in office, but whose ability to deal with troublemakers is sometimes uncanny. They monitored a senior delegate from the FUT for a trial period of a week.

On the first day the delegate began the morning shift in the full kit as detailed in the regulations, although at close of play the raincoat was left at the worksite because, in the estimation of the delegate, it wasn't raining.

The rest of the clothing was dried during the evening as reports continued to come in of state-wide flooding. Several towns had been washed away and many people had been tragically buried by hailstones. On the second morning, management provided another coat from a secret supply in the boardroom as driving rain was still falling and only the tops of the trees were visible. Although it touched the ground and was described by the delegate as "a hideous boring tent", the coat looked well with the hat, and it also matched the one boot that was found.

By the beginning of day four, the boot position had been clarified to the point where each foot had a boot and one of the boots bore the name of the delegate. Another boot was found in the delegate's bag but even the National Union of Grandparents couldn't work out whose it was or how it had got there. An office-bearer in the Massed Fives suggested that the boot may have been put there by Martians, as apparently something very similar had just happened on television.

A marked shortage of socks on the fifth morning occasioned a search of the dormitory zone. Those involved are still only learning to talk about it. Things were seen which beggar the imagination and reveal much about the so-called 'dark side' of the human soul.

On the plus side, the second coat was found rolled up under a bookshelf and inside it were two pairs of socks, a yoghurt container full of deceased moths and an apple that has been carbon-dated to the early 1520s. The matter of the bicycle wheel and the object which may have been a sea-anenome was dealt with separately and I'll say no more about it here. It has not been an easy time for us and it is with high heart that we anticipate the prospect of spring.

There will be more rain of course. Farmers need rain. And it affords the Massed Five-Year-Olds a wonderful opportunity to get out in their new hat, new coat and brand new gumboots; especially now they've finished the dinosaur book.

Golf

A series of golf lessons with the Great White Whale, one of the true legends of the game. As a player he thrilled a generation, playing shots of astonishing power and virtuosity, many of them unusual and some of them not previously thought possible.

Hi there! I thought we'd begin with a few general things which might be of use to the weekend golfer, because when you think about it, most golfers are not playing in big tournaments. The vast majority of golfers are simply people who like to get out and hit a ball.

It's a great game, as we all know. Let's see if we can improve our performances by remembering a few basic rules. I can't offer a guarantee of course, but these are the questions I'm most often asked about.

Playing the Shot

It is important to lift your head as you hit the ball. This ensures control and frequently improves distance. Also, if you keep your head down you won't see where you have hit the ball. The result is that you will lose the ball and, of course, you can't play the game without one.

I played with a young fellow recently who kept his head down for every single shot. He literally never knew where his ball had gone. Fortunately, I was able to find it for him quite often on the green or in the hole, but what he does when I'm not there I shudder to think.

Stance

Very important. The correct stance is obviously crucial. The exact position is up to you. Make sure you are comfortable. Although don't make the mistake of sitting down.

There are two main positions relative to the ball:

(a) Too close, and

(b) Too far away.

Many experienced players combine them. They stand too far from the ball, hit it, and then find that they are standing too close to it.

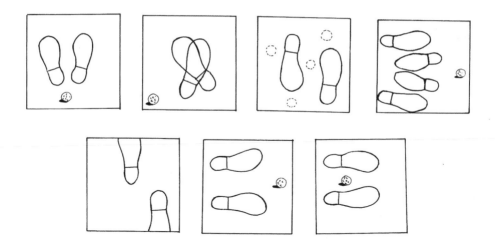

A Few Simple Tips

Here are some little pointers which I have found very helpful over the years.

- If your ball is in trouble, shift it.
- If there is water to the left of the fairway and safety to the right, don't take silly risks. Pull your front foot back about 45 centimetres and hit your ball into the water.
- When you fail to get your weight through the ball properly, get your confidence back by banging the club repeatedly on the ground.

Putting

Putting is a separate game and there are as many putting styles as there are individual players. My own putting action might not work for anyone else. It doesn't work for me. Why the hell it should work for anyone else I can't imagine.

PUTT-ING ON THE RITZ

Scoring

Don't worry about how you are scoring. Why put pressure on yourself? Just concentrate on your shots. At the end of the round, look over the card and score yourself along the following lines.

A drive that hit a tree, second shot never found, a couple of other shots and four putts: Score Par.

A good drive, a second shot which would be on the green if the wind hadn't hauled it on to the next fairway, two third shots and an approach to within 12 metres of the flag: Score Par.

A magnificent drive, long second shot into light rough, short third into heavy rough, a bit of tidying up, some approach shots and a few putts: Score Bogey [the penalty for a lapse in concentration].

Twelve shots to the green and one putt: Score Bogey [good recovery].

Hit the green in one, eight putts: Score Bogey.

Hit the carpark in one, took a drop, shanked ball into nearby lake, took a drop, drove beyond the green, missed it coming back, overhit gentle pitch-and-run, misread difficult lie down bank and lofted ball into sprinkler-housing on adjacent fairway, took a drop, missed ball altogether, moved it with foot, topped it into long grass, took a drop, troubled by low branches affecting swing, threw ball on to green, hit green with second throw, missed long putt by centimetres, missed next two attempts and tapped in with toe of shoe: Score Double Bogey. Make mental note to be careful on this hole next time.

LITTLE WAY   FAIR WAY

Enjoying Your Golf

One of the great things about golf is the opportunity it affords to simply get outside and enjoy the world we live in. The best time to appreciate the world we live in is about halfway through your downswing. As you feel the clubhead beginning to accelerate towards the ball, pull your face up and have a good look at the surrounding countryside. Some regular players have trained themselves to study cloud formations as the ball is actually being struck.

WATER HAZARD

The Grip

Many players have a reasonable swing but they throw it away with a bad grip. A hook or a slice can often be traced to a grip problem.

The correct grip is the Double-Latice Multi-Stress Underlap grip in which the fingers of the left or leading hand are wound beneath the thumb of the right hand at the point where it crosses an imaginary line drawn from the base of the clubhead through the apex of the shoulder at the top of the backswing, although obviously you do that the other way round if you're left-handed and, of course, you reverse that if you're not.

The grip should be firm. There's nothing worse than playing an important shot and looking up to see your club disappearing over a big clump of conifers because you weren't holding on to it properly.

Your arms should feel nice and strong, there should be plenty of tension across the back of the shoulders, your hands and wrists should be rigid with that potential energy and strength, and you should be able to see your knuckles going white with exertion and concentration. If your knuckles aren't white, perhaps golf isn't your game.

Imagine the Shot

Many famous golfers recommend 'picturing' each shot; imagining a 'film' of the shot being played. This is a useful technique and should be adopted whenever possible. Look at the shot. Imagine it being played. 'See' it in your 'mind'.

Then go home. Do not attempt to play the shot.

Bunker Shots

Don't 'psyche yourself out'. Assess the position carefully, with a positive outlook and a specific aim. Work out where you would like the ball to land. Then take a sand wedge, work your feet into the ground slightly to give yourself some traction, take a couple of practice swings and then pick the ball up and throw it on to the green.

Club Selection

It is important when selecting a club to be aware of the distance it is designed to hit. Let's have a look in the bag. Let's say you're playing a relatively standard par 4; it's 412 metres from tee to green with bunkers left and right at about 238 metres, water down the left side and a forest to the right containing a number of tigers.

From the tee you'll need distance. A driver, a 1 wood or a 2 wood should get you over most of the trouble; ideally over the bunkers although, personally, I'd be just as happy to be over the water or over the tigers. As long as you get over something.

Your next shot, not counting a bit of cleaning up here and there, your next shot of any real importance is very often a remarkable recovery shot and frequently requires a good lusty whack of about 183 metres. There are two ways to approach this: you can try to get to the green with, say, a 3 iron or you can pull out the fairway wood and lay up, leaving yourself a pitch of about 170 metres.

Around the green the sand wedge comes into its own. This club is particularly useful for players who enjoy looking at flags. Get the flag lined up properly, try to guess how far away it is and whether the fact that it's fluttering has anything to do with the wind. Look up at it and shift your feet a few times, then look at it again in case it moved while you were shifting your feet. Now shorten the backswing slightly and play a fairly simple little pitch, looking at the flag as you commence the downswing. Don't worry about the ball, you can find that in a minute, it won't have gone far.

One further word about clubs: two of the most valuable clubs in the game, you have on your feet. You can very often solve quite difficult problems, which baffle less skilled golfers, by playing a judicious pitch with the foot-iron. You will sometimes see a golfer standing under a low branch of a tree, bent double and with no room for a backswing, or obliged to chop a ball out of some grassy hollow with no view of the green. These golfers are only fooling themselves. Believe me, there are no shortcuts; if you want to play the game properly, you need the right equipment.

Here are the distances you ought to be looking for with each club in your bag.

DRIVER WOOD

Driver: Anywhere from 1 to 450 metres in pretty well any direction.

3 wood: 13 metres.

1 iron: There is no such thing as a 1 iron.

2 iron: Difficult to tell. No one has ever found a shot hit with a 2 iron.

3 iron: 165–180 metres in regions where there are no trees.

4 iron: Exactly the same as a 3 iron or a 5 iron.

5 iron: 130–550 metres, mainly to the right.

6 iron: For playing a 5 iron shot with the wind behind you or a 7 iron shot which you wish to hook into oncoming traffic.

7 iron: 140 metres. Annually.

8 iron: 120–135 metres unless there is water within 18 metres.

9 iron: Just short of any distance.

Pitching wedge: See Driver.

Sand wedge: 75–125 millimetres.

IRON

Practice

How often do I practise? I don't, but of course I'm not typical. I've reached a kind of Zen plateau where I no longer need to practise. I have a couple of general swings on the first tee with one of the longer irons, just to get the feeling back in my joints, but otherwise I seem to be beyond the stage where mere practice is of any real use.

I do sometimes practise an individual shot. For instance, if I detect a slight swing-fault with my driver, the first ball I hit is frequently a practice shot and I don't start scoring until I get my rhythm right and hit a decent one.

In the case of chipping it is sometimes necessary to hit three or four practice balls before getting one to work. Obviously if the first ball runs up to the hole nicely there is no need to improve the shot and you should simply move on.

Putting practice can improve your score by several strokes and I recommend it be incorporated in every golfer's routine. The best time to practise your putting is immediately after you have putted, while the fault is still fresh in your mind. Put another ball down and have another try. Many golfers practise putting BEFORE THEY START PLAYING. I have never seen much mileage in this, since it is not clear until you are playing your round exactly what the fault might be, if any. Why sap your confidence by assuming that some of your putts won't go in? I stand up to every shot on the course believing it will go in the hole. I don't play a shot until I am convinced in my own mind it will go in. I hate to think what my score would be if I faced reality prior to making contact with the ball. I may well go to pieces.

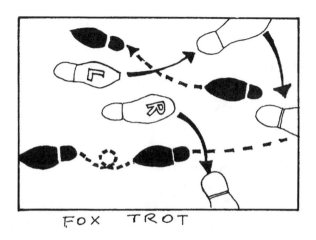

FOX TROT

The Tempo of the Swing

The rhythm, or TEMPO, of your golf swing is crucial. If you are rushing your shots or trying to force the ball, the chances are control will be lost and your game will deteriorate. Each player has a different swing and no two TEMPOS are the same.

In fact, I quite often use a different TEMPO for every shot. I have been asked about this many times and, although I have never listed my various TEMPOS before, it may help some struggling golfers to know that I have at least five main ones:

1. Very slow and deliberate takeaway, holding the club at the top of the backswing for a moment to steady the shot and then swinging through the ball at the speed of sound. Useful in all conditions and a TEMPO I personally favour.

2. Beginning the downswing before the backswing is completed and stopping the clubhead as it hits the ball. This eliminates the need for transferral of weight and minimises the importance of club selection.

3. Extremely long takeaway, forcing the upper part of the body well back so you can almost see underneath the ball, and then, at some instinctive signal from the brain, jumping into the shot and driving the clubhead powerfully up the front of the ball and into a follow-through of astonishing velocity.

4. Lifting the club away more or less vertically and then slamming it down on to the very back of the ball and through into the layers of rich loam that lie many hundreds of metres under the earth's surface.

5. Taking the clubhead away inside the line and starting the downswing with a forward thrust of the hips and a simultaneous lifting of the front shoulder which takes the club back outside the line from the top of the swing but inside the line again once the drive from the back leg pushes the hands ahead of the ball with the uncocking of the wrists and the acceleration of the clubhead itself pulls the hands, the back elbow and the ball into alignment for the moment of impact. This TEMPO is not easy to repeat at will and I personally have only ever achieved it once. I was attempting a number 1 but was surprised by a sprinkler system at an important point in the downswing.

Now go out and shoot a 63.

What you do on the second hole is up to you.

AUSTRALIAFORM

1 July 1989 to 30 June 1990

Specify period if part year or approved substitute period.

Post or deliver the return by 31 August 1990 to a Taxation Office in the State in which the income was derived or was last seen.

This document must be carried at all times while the driver is in charge of a car on any public highway.

IMPORTANT

Please complete Section [A] before moving on to Sections [B] [C] [D] and [E].
You must answer one question from Section [B] or [C] and one each from Sections [D] [E] and [P] before returning to the Optional Sheet [attached].
If you require more paper, raise your hand and ask the supervisor.
You may start writing now.

SECTION [A]   ▲
SURNAME . . . .
GIVEN NAME . . . .
(If Keating or Howard, move to Section [F])
Personal tax number (Confidential) . . . .
[Will not be revealed to anyone who does not already have it]   ★★★★★★★★★★★★★★★★★★★★

Name of spouse. . . . .
Maiden name of spouse . . . .
[Where applicable]   ■ ■ ■ ■
Does/do Spouse/es Fill in His/Her/Its/Their [if more than one] Form or does/do Spouse/es consent willingly and/or freely to his/her/its/their [if more than one] details being included herein. Such consent to be represented by the affixing of his/her/ its/their [if more than one] signature/s [if more than one].
Names of children. . . . .
Your own children. Do not attempt to be amusing in any way   ▶

ADDRESS. . . . .
Address to which bills and court summons may be sent. . . . .

Occupation (if any) . . . .
Other occupations. . . . .
Occupations not mentioned so far . . . .
                                                                                ▼
Have you had anything to drink in the last 4 hours?. . . . . YES/NO
Are you a member of an approved superannuation scheme?. . . . . YES/NO
Well don't worry, we'll get you anyway.   ❑ ■

INCOME   ▲
What was your income during the year to June 30? . . . .
How was it obtained? . . . .
Where is it now?. . . . .
Who touched it last? . . . .
Have you conducted a thorough search around the home? . . . .
What did it look like? . . . .

Have you reported the loss? . . . .

Was your income gross? . . . .

VERY ☐ UNBELIEVABLY ☐ I AM A DOCTOR ☐

Enter subtotal here

Carry forward amount [G] net of depreciation

Add on Items 7,18, 26 and Part xxi from Heading M.

Attach sheets 8–34

Pin tax stamps to back of earning statement and retire to safe distance

Show accrued yields from all interest sources as per Section T

Add money left in other trousers, down back of carseat, in jar on mantlepiece, glovebox, other [specify]

Imputed amount for enjoyment of garden or reading

Express checkout: 8 items or less   ◄ ◄ ◄

SECTION T   ▲

Income from other sources . . . .

Name Race Meeting . . . .

Date of Race Meeting . . . .

Nature of Investment . . . . , ...

State Odds . . . .

Did you witness race in Question? . . . . .Why not? . . . .

State name of brother-in-law . . . .

Amount consumed . . . .

Furnish recording of brother-in-law singing *Danny Boy*   ◄━━━━━━━━━━

SECTION [B]   ▲

Company return . . . .

Address of registered office . . . .

Company file number . . . .

[Cannot be used except by persons who read this document or data sourced from this document. Staff of The Taxation Office and their families are not eligible to enter this competition]

    i What books of account, if any, are kept by or on behalf of the taxpayer? . . . .

    ii By whom are these books kept? . . . .

    iii Where is he? . . . .

    iv Would you recognise him if you saw him again? . . . .

    v Is the return in accordance with those books? . . . .

    vi If the return is not in accordance with those books, which books is the return in accordance with? . . . .

    vii Have the film-rights been sold? . . . .

    viii If this return has been prepared by an Accountant, has this Accountant ever won a major award for Fiction? . . . .

    ix Is the Accountant in Jail? . . . .

LIST OF SHAREHOLDERS   ■ ■ ■

Living . . . .

Non-living . . . .

Other . . . .

WHERE WERE YOU ON 17 OCTOBER 1987?

. . . .

OK LET'S TALK ABOUT SOMETHING ELSE   ✪

LEAVE BLANK

APPROVED DEDUCTIONS   ▲
Office Expenses, School fees, Travel and Accommodation, Equipment. Stationery, Depreciation,
Furniture and fittings, Sex, Bribes to Law Enforcement Personnel, Wastage [Ariadne Shares, Liberal
Party Donations etc]. . . . .
Other . . . .

See Box [7] Under GENERAL   ❾

DO NOT WRITE IN THIS BOX   →

OR THIS ONE   ←

Key to symbols
AO Adults only. PGR – Parental Guidance Recommended. . . . .
G General Viewing . . . .
ABC Repeat

SECTION [Y]   ▲
Indemnity
IS THE ABOVE A VOLUNTARY STATEMENT? . . . .
HAS ANY THREAT, INDUCEMENT OR PROMISE BEEN HELD OUT TO YOU TO MAKE
THIS STATEMENT? . . . .
DO YOU SEE THAT MAN IN COURT? . . . .
DO YOU WISH TO HAVE THE CONTINENTAL BREAKFAST? . . . .

SECTION [F]
To be completed if your name is Keating or Howard.

Name . . . .
Last return lodged . . . .
PLEASE BE SERIOUS
Address. . . . .
Other address. . . . .

DO YOU THINK THIS IS FAIR? . . . .   ●

SCORE THE FOLLOWING STATEMENTS IN ORDER OF PREFERENCE 1–5   ●
I enjoy the company of others
I enjoy the company of some others
I enjoy the company of other companies
I find it difficult to build up a rapport with others
By and large people give me the squirts   ■

The Trickle-Down Effect is   ●
a] A process whereby money given to the rich trickles down to the poor.
b] A process whereby instructions given by the rich trickle down to the government.
c] A code name for the Trickle-Up Effect.

ACCOUNTANTS

If you are filling this form in for a client or friend, should you have one, you must complete this section.

Name . . . .

Name of person for whom you are filling in this form . . . .

Is he/she in the room with you? . . . .

What fee are you charging? . . . .

Pardon? . . . .

Will you get away with it? . . . .

Have you got away with it before? . . . .

How many times have you got away with it? . . . .

Sorry I can hardly hear you

Is your client sane? 32u

⊔⊔⊔

Part 4[b]   ▲

If you answered "yes" to question 20 or "don't know" to either question 17 or 24 [in section 12 on P.5] complete the following very carefully

  i] Is the discharge coloured?

  ii] How many sex partners have you had in the last month?

  iii] Name them. Male. . . . . Female. . . . .

      Other [specify] . . . .

      Extra space is available on the reverse

  iv] It's for their own good

  v] Look at the photographs in Schedule 9

  vi] Memory perked up a bit now has it?

 viii] Cough

  ix] Do you suffer from any of the following

      Hepatitis, Gall Stones, Corked thigh, Pulled giblets, Dipsotryponia, Telecom Business Services, General anxiety, Hearing voices, Paranoia.

SECTION J

G   What City are the 2000 Sydney Olympics being held in? . . . .

E   Why? . . . .

H   Who are the Aborigines? . . . .

A   What are The Arts? . . . .

SN   What Rain Forest has a new road through it? . . . .

SL   Who runs Australia when the Head of the Casino has the day off? . . . .

SECTION K   ▲

Did you get a pension during the year to June 30? . . . .

Type of Pension? . . . .

Which war? . . . .

Do you think anyone cares? . . . .

Who cares? . . . .

We need names . . . .

Can you walk? . . . .

Well, can you hop? . . . .

Do you think complaining is part of the Great Australian Tradition? . . . .

Goodness gracious me

Words fail me   ©

Carefully insert flap [f] into socket [j] folding along line p-q to meet at housing [d] and invert reverse section at [t] to rest on pinion [h] using tube of glue provided. ❏

DECLARATION

I declare that the particulars in this return are true, certainly as true as anyone else's, and that they provide a fair to reasonable impression of the overall picture taking into consideration a margin for error and not counting the odd thing I may have overlooked in the rush to get this in on time, or very nearly. I am over 18 or accompanied by an adult.

Signature . . . . Date . . . .

REGARDLESS OF YOUR TAX OBLIGATION, DO YOU WISH TO MAKE A DONATION ANYWAY?

Yes. . . . . No. . . . . Other. . . . .

[specify]   3n

THINK ABOUT IT

I understand that I pay NOTHING for 6 weeks but that after that I'll be peddling like a duck.

✂ - ◄

CUSTOMER SERVICE DIVISION

Helping us to serve you

1. Where did you first hear about the Australian Taxation Office?
❏ Read an advertisement.

❏ Saw one of your boards on a building.

❏ Was told about it by friends.

❏ Attended a mortgagee sale.

2. How would you rate the service you received?
❏ Excellent   ❏ Fabulous

❏ Friendly and helpful   ❏ Post-modern .

❏ Refreshingly efficient.

| OFFICE USE ONLY |

Customer description: Action taken:
❏ Compulsive liar   ❏ Cleaned him/her out

❏ Muddler but not criminal   ❏ Summons issued

❏ Unctuous buffoon   ❏ Other[specify] . . . .

❏ Complete mongrel   ❏ Other[specify] . . . .

89/90

Australia and How to Repair It

In case of fire break glass.

Operational Manual

Congratulations. You are a part-owner of 'Australia' [TM] a fully-serviced time-share resort and manufacturing centre set in the attractive environs of South East Asia. [Still Selling but Hurry.]

We trust you will be satisfied with your 'State' [TM] and that you have noted the names of participating dealers in your 'City' [TM].

Despite the best traditions and the highest standards of design and maintenance, management wishes to advise that owners may experience some minor problems. 'Australia [TM] is still in the early stages of development and many teething troubles require constant attention.

During the past year, for instance, head office has been inundated with calls from people complaining that they had been charged for a Bicentennial but had not received one. In fact, only the 'Sydney' [TM] Model was fitted with a Bicentennial money-tap and the function has now been discontinued for obvious reasons.

A slight fault in the wiring of the Economics display-screen has been discovered and it is with regret that we announce the overall position is somewhat less attractive than we may have indicated. Notice the position of the mustering station nearest to your seat.

Due to an increasing number of calls to our offices, it has been decided to produce a guide to the Use and Care of 'Australia' [TM]. May we suggest you keep the guide near the unit at all times.

Should a problem emerge, refer to the guide and apply the remedy outlined in the handy-to-use table. If pain persists, see a doctor.

Troubleshooting

PROBLEM	PROBABLE CAUSE	WHAT TO DO
GRAUNCHING SOUND COMING FROM TREASURY	Balance of Payments valve clogged.	This problem may be accompanied by sparks from the back of the main panel and an increase in the Hawke sports-photograph syndrome. Turn unit off at wall. Check use-by date on budgetry estimates. Place bucket under explanation printout tray, open Keating-filter and leave overnight. Have area sprayed in morning.
SPORTING RESULTS NOT WHAT THEY WERE IN THE 1950s. VERY COMMON COMPLAINT IN THE HOSPITALITY INDUSTRY.	It is the 1980s.	Come to terms with Probable Cause. Have a nice day.
GREENHOUSE EFFECT	Greed.	Nothing
THE ARTS	Need to keep unemployment confined to lower section of batting order.	Spend small fraction of cost of National Tennis Centre. Make speech: 'Vital We Retain Distinctive Cultural Identity'. Give money to Bureaucrats.

Troubleshooting

PROBLEM	PROBABLE CAUSE	WHAT TO DO
AUSTRALIAN LITERATURE' [TM]	Misreading of Handbook. 'Australian Literature' [TM] is not a Pleasure Function. See Bourgeois.	Plug the Old Friends and Relations Pin into the back of the Funding Network Job Inventor. Fold results back into Private Production Opening. Suck gently on Literature Board Valve until flow is regulated, then direct into Publishing Output Mode. Pull Premier's Award Knob until fully extended and allow Favours and Tradeoff Sacks to empty. If Loss Quotient unacceptable, push Tax Flusher and open Development Grant Function. Key in Personal Bank Account Digit Number. Enter Password. [Try 'Quality and Innovation'.] Put name at bottom of list and send to four people you went to school with.
THE ABC	He's just popped out for a moment or two. He was here a minute ago.	Someone will get back to you later today. Friday. Monday at the very latest.
BANK PROFITS AT ALARMING LEVELS	Secrecy-screen not working. Truth leaking through code de-scrambler. Check Hawke posturing switch.	Increase Home Lending rates. Slap thigh.

Troubleshooting

PROBLEM	PROBABLE CAUSE	WHAT TO DO
LIBERAL PARTY FAILS TO OPERATE. EMITS CONTINUOUS MOAN	Howard-eject button jammed.	Locate wiring to back up decoy. Re-route power-lead to spring-loaded hinges on far right of central dingbattery. Pull Chaney-supply cord from upper housing and plug into lower socket. Cross fingers. Guess own weight.
THE PRESS	Too great a diversity of Ownership.	Open back of Government section. Pull out Media Legislation panel. Take central decision-making mechanism and plug into money-fellation unit. Obtain paper through completely independent paper-supply feeder at rear of money-fellation unit. Enter facts into PR convertor attached to money-fellation unit. Read printout into money-fellation recorder. Caution: if competition indicator blinks, turn off immediately and replace roll.

Troubleshooting

PROBLEM	PROBABLE CAUSE	WHAT TO DO
TELEPHONE SERVICES CHARGED FOR BUT UNAVAILABLE	Loose connection between Telecom profit accelerator and actual usefulness counter.	Call service department. Please enjoy the music.
CPI SENDING BACK PHOTOGRAPHS OF OTHER SIDE OF MOON	The industrial output flow-pipe has been wrongly labelled in the manual of the Keating.	The industrial output flow-pipe has been wrongly labelled in the manual of the Keating Deluxe model. Subsequently redesignated '24 hour constant industrial in-flow tube'. This was not picked up earlier due to a distortion in commodity prices. We apologise for any inconvenience. If the unit was purchased from 'Creans' [The Working Man's Friend] it is unfortunately out of warranty.
QUEENSLAND	Unknown but it looks bad, Your Honour.	500 units. Detective Sergeant Simpson. Race 4.
HOUSE PRICES	Share prices.	Share Houses.

Troubleshooting

PROBLEM	PROBABLE CAUSE	WHAT TO DO
JOHN DAWKINS	Liked his education so much he bought the company.	Answer all questions. [1] If a student cannot afford his/her University fees he/she will a) Take in washing. b) Mow lawns. c) Pick up a little baby-sitting work. d) Sell drugs. [2] The drugs will be sold a) Around the family home. b) Around the House of Representatives. c) Around the Mulberry Bush. d) Around the University. [3] Make up own question. Mark out of 100. Enclose fee.
CHILD POVERTY	Adult Poverty.	Bob will eliminate child poverty by 1990. Please enjoy the music.

Warranty and Conditions Attaching to Citizenship

The CITIZEN hereby warrants that any or all complaints referred to herein are genuine and bona fide and have been witnessed by authorised persons or their agents.

All information provided hereintofore is fair and reasonable and all goods were checked by suitably trained artisans upon despatch and/or transmission.

No CITIZEN will at any time speak in a manner likely to bring discredit or opprobrium on this his/her native/adopted wide/brown/other [specify] land in any wise and in any capacity unless said person is an imbecile or a member of Her Majesty's Opposition.

The penalties for abuses or breaches of this or any other Regulation in whole or in part shall be those laid down in The Crimes Act [Sundry Complaints Division] 1927 [and subsequent amendments] taking into consideration those writs in accordance with Normal Redress in Matters of Umbrage, Dudgeon and Righteousness, the Treatment of Pelts by Minors, Claims against the State by Individuals Not Yet Born (R v. Jung), the Statutory Maintenance of Sealanes and other concerns bearing in material detail on the case WITH THE SINGLE EXCEPTION of Writs in Fee Complicit. These shall be deemed to include; Claims by a Shire against itself, Claims by Drivers against Roadways and Sidings (SRA v. Moss), Claims by Buildings against Architects or their agents, and Claims involving two foreign nations (W. Indies v. Pakistan). WHERE the State Boundaries are those determined by Ordnance Survey No. 73982 and $\pi = 22/7$.

Those CITIZENS sniggering at the back will stay behind afterwards and see Mr Richardson.

The CITIZEN agrees that this country [hereinafter referred to as The Entire Joint] is in GOOD and CAPABLE hands and is superbly managed in every way and that any problems and/or breakdowns due to equipment failure or negligence of any type whatsoever are THE SOLE AND COMPLETE RESPONSIBILITY of the CITIZEN and are nothing to do with the Government and are specifically nothing to do with Robert Jesus Lee Hawke, THE PEOPLE'S CHOICE [all stand] who has at all times struggled to carry the difficult load of office and has done so most NOBLY under very bloody difficult circumstances.

The CITIZEN furthermore warrants and UNDERTAKES TO KEEP

WARRANTING that whatever the apparent failings of Paul Keating, WHICH ARE ONLY VERY SLIGHT IF THEY EXIST AT ALL, there is and can be no doubt whatsoever in the mind of a reasonable person that HE IS VERY GOOD AT WHAT HE DOES. The names of the people he has done it to can be inspected during normal business hours at the office of any Parisian tailor.

Someone will get back to you. Please enjoy the music.

Position Position Position Position Position Position Position Position

A U S T R A L I A

FOR SALE. BEST WE'VE SEEN.
MORTGAGEE'S SALE. RENOVATOR'S DREAM.

Rare opp to purch lge rmblng home and bus. Beautifully sitd on hge blck. Estab trees. Cls shps, schls, transpt. D/Htg. Flly sewered and cln as whstl. Prop has been in hands vend 200 yrs. Early hmstd. subseq renov incl Federation style, Victrn, Edwdn, Spnsh, Gk, Ital, Viet. All wk qual crftsmn. Finished to exctg stds.

Main bldgs great histor intrst. Replumbed, rewired, reblocked, 70s. Approx 17mill sqs. Compr oodles bdrms wi excell feats. Many with ensuite. BIRs. Master opens to swpng ver. Formal sittngrm. OFP wi mrble mantle. Sep form dinrm. OFP. Lge recptn rm opening to superb tce wi pergola and vistas hills, bush, home to num birds, wals, kos, kangs, rch tpstry nat faun, poss sml num ven tds, snks, crcdls.

Fam rm feats qual chats, drapes, fttngs, WW carps. Lge mod elec ktchn. Imported Miele b'fast area, Ital tiles out to balc. Exec bthrm, sep shwr, Sep WC. Sep lndry recntly refurbd, groaning wi period feats. Rumpus rm o'looks patio and rear crtyd wi lmtlss OS prkg.

Granny flts wi u/flr htg, ceil roses, strnge wll hgngs and pctrs grdchldn arsl/brkfst.

Lge area at rear. Approx 7.5mill sq km. Rm N/S Tns crt. Rm spa/IG pool. Suit animals. 800mill dse. Mny outbldgs wi loads chrm. Beaut bung (roof needs work). Stables converted cabana/loft for mod lux soph lvg. Hydronic htg. ROW at rear. Also old fact, orig feats, once prod manuf gds, some rust in doors and roof, fab opp refurb or convert units, poss tourism $, subj council approv. L/U accom for lcl popltn.

Conven resid locn, pop wi chldrn, Magnif views fr lfty pks (lnd grt by sea) in much sought-after snbrnt cntry, lnd swping plns, rggd mtn rngs, d's, fldg r's.

Curr mngt nt vry brght. As reslt prop not comm viable. Owner says must sell. Insp by appt only.

A/H Toshi Watanabe 8813542
A/H Hiram W Mouthguard III 8730995

Stage
Royal Commission
1991

A Royal Commission into the Australian Economy

*The following is an extract from the stage production of the
Royal Commission into the Australian Economy, co-written with
Ross Stevenson, which opened at the Belvoir Street Theatre in Sydney
in March 1991. Another production opened in Melbourne in April and
another in Adelaide, which toured to regional centres. It was later
produced for television.*

*The set was a court-room and the Commission had the power to call
anyone in the country in an attempt to find out what had gone wrong
with the economy. Evidence was given by captains of industry, bank
chiefs, union bosses, the Prime Minister and a great many worthwhile
people as well. The evidence of Alan Bond and Mr Trouser, an official
in the Treasury, were particularly telling. Of course, as you will see,
none of this could happen in New Zealand.*

A short primate enters and walks to the box. He is handed a Bible. He looks at it and puts it in his pocket. He winks at counsel assisting the Commission, Mr Malcolm Turnbull.

Turnbull: Mr Bond, thank you for your time.
Bond: Thank you, Malcolm. [To the Judge.] Your Worship.
Judge: I'm Your Honour, Mr Bond.
Bond: I beg yours?
Judge: I'm Your Honour.
Bond: No, you've lost me.
Judge: The proper form of address for a judge is "Your Honour".
Bond: Oh.
Turnbull: Mr Bond. This Inquiry has heard evidence today of the vital role played in the Australian economy during the 1980s by the major corporate figures. You are a businessman?
Bond: No, I'm an entrepreneur.
Turnbull: I understood you were a businessman.
Judge: What's the difference?
Bond: A businessman runs a business, Your Airship.
Turnbull: What does an entrepreneur do?

Bond: He does what he likes, Mr Turnbull.

Turnbull: And have you been successful?

Bond: As an entrepreneur?

Turnbull: Yes.

Bond: Very successful, thank you.

Turnbull: And as a businessman?

Bond: I'm not a businessman, Mr Turnbull. I'm an entrepreneur.

Turnbull: What did you do? Did you develop remarkable new overseas markets for Australian goods? Did you secure long-term foreign investment finance for new industries? [Bond clearly doesn't understand.] Something easier to start with Mr Bond? Did you develop new overseas markets . . .

Bond: No, we bought companies that had assets capable of generating greater profits than they were. Australian business was very inefficient.

Turnbull: So you purchased these companies and, using superior management skills, you made them perform . . .

Judge: . . . Increasing your own profits but building a more vigorous industry, with sound policy settings, generating new employment and investment opportunities and contributing taxation monies to the general pool for the greater good of society.

Bond: No, if it's got assets worth 50 million but it's only valued at 28 million, you find buyers for the assets, borrow 28, pull the 50 and stick 22 million in your pocket.

Judge: Don't you have to pay back the interest on the money you borrowed to do it?

Bond: No. You declare your profit and shares in your company go up as people scramble to get on board. So now your company is worth more.

Turnbull: What does your company produce?

Bond: You're producing profits, this is the point. Your share price goes up and your company is worth more money and you can borrow more.

Judge: Why is your company worth more money Mr Bond? You haven't produced anything and you still owe the interest on the loan you took out in the first place.

Bond: Would you mind not interrupting all the time? This enables you to borrow more and buy another company, so you do that and declare an even BIGGER profit, so your share price goes up again. Ours got to $12.50 at one stage.

Judge: What is it now?

Bond: No, you're missing the point, Your Worship. You start buying overseas, you diversify, you buy media, you buy minerals, you buy brewing, you're everywhere.

Judge: And how big are your borrowings at this point?

Bond: You just roll your borrowings over. That's not a problem. Normal business practice.

Turnbull: I thought you said you weren't a businessman, Mr Bond.

Judge: But isn't all this based on your share price? You haven't mentioned paying back any of the loans. Do the people who are buying your shares know how much you owe?

Bond: Listen, I'm trying to give you the big picture here! Will you let me finish something? You're ruining my flow. And you don't want to get too worried about borrowings, Your Highness. Bear in mind that if people are getting a quid they don't pull you up about the paperwork.

Judge: Yes. A wise old adage Mr Bond and thank you for sharing it with us. My point is that your borrowings are only manageable so long as your share price is high, and your share price will only be high so long as no one finds out about your borrowings. This is not a sound, logical way to proceed and it cannot possibly be good business.

Bond: I'm not a businessman. I'm an entrepreneur.

Turnbull: Mr Bond, when you take over a company that isn't performing and sell its assets, what happens to the company?

Bond: It's not there any more.

Turnbull: What about the buildings?

Bond: Sold.

Judge: What about the people who worked there?

Bond: Gone.

Judge: These people who have gone, Mr Bond. Where did they go?

Bond: I don't know. I'm not a travel agent.

Judge: You don't know where they are? How many of them are there?

Bond: Oh it varies. In the case of Waltons there were about 2000.

Turnbull: Presumably they either get other jobs or receive the unemployment benefit.

Bond: Not really my department, Mr Turnbull.

Turnbull: Two thousand people tipped out of work by you. They are now receiving unemployment benefits totalling $300,000 a week, paid for by the taxpayer.

Bond: Not my area, I'm afraid.

Judge: At the risk of interrupting your flow, Mr Bond, this money you borrow. Do you borrow it overseas?

Bond: Some of it

Judge: How much?

Bond: About six billion.

Judge: So that would show up in Australia's Current Account?

Bond: Not really my department, Your Eminence.

Turnbull: How much tax do you pay?

Bond: In Australia?

Turnbull: Yes.

Bond: I don't pay tax in Australia. My company is incorporated in the Cook Islands.

Turnbull: How much tax do you pay in the Cook Islands?

Bond: The Cook Islands don't have any tax.

Turnbull: The Chairman of Elders has been quoted as saying "Some of my friends don't even pay tax". Do you know Mr Elliott?

Bond: Yes. He's a friend of mine.

Turnbull: Mr Bond, if you made a profit it was declared in the Cook Islands, where there is no tax. If you made a loss it was, no doubt, declared in Australia. Your expenses too, I would suggest, were incurred in Australia.

Bond: Correct weight, Malcolm.

Judge: Mr Bond. Just explain to me. Aside from this impeccable record in the taxation area, what exactly are your successes? Just take us through some selected highlights of your achievements.

Bond: I started in Property Development in Western Australia and I moved into resources, I bought all of South Australia's Gas in 1981, I bought Swan Brewing, I bought Channel 9, I bought an airship company, I bought Waltons, I bought hotels, I bought a university, I got down on some art, all good stuff, no rubbish. I won the America's Cup in 1983.

Turnbull: The America's Cup. And how did that improve companies that weren't performing?

Bond: Well you get very popular all of a sudden, politicians climbing up your arse. I had a Prime Minister stuck to my sleeve for about two years. If a photographer turned up he'd get a plane from Canberra; I couldn't get rid of him.

Turnbull: How does this help you? Having an elected public official down your trousers.

Bond: Oh it's unbelievable. It opens doors all over the world. They love sport, businessmen.

Judge: Do you like sport?

Bond: I'm an entrepreneur, Jana.

Turnbull: Did your share price go up, Mr Bond?

Bond: Went through the roof, Your Excellency.

Judge: And did you pay back the money you'd borrowed to buy all the things you have just listed?

Bond: No. I borrowed an extra $4 billion.

Judge: Silly me.

Turnbull: You mentioned art, Mr Bond. What art did you buy?

Bond: I didn't buy any art. I got hold of a painting called "Irises" by Van Gogh but I didn't buy it.

Judge: Where did you get it?

Bond: I got it from Sothebys who are a high-class secondhand outfit. Paintings and old chairs and stuff.

Turnbull: What did it cost?

Bond: Fifty-seven million dollars.

Turnbull: You didn't buy it. How did you have it if you didn't buy it?

Bond: Sothebys lent me the money. It cost $57 million but I didn't pay Sothebys $57 million. I paid them the interest on $57 million.

Turnbull: Sothebys sold the painting to themselves. Why did they do that?

Bond: To make it look as if paintings were selling for very large amounts of money.

Turnbull: Why did they do that?

Bond: Because they're in the business of selling paintings for very large amounts of money.

Judge: As a matter of interest, why is "Irises" so expensive? Why is it more expensive, for instance, than Leonardo Da Vinci's "Mona Lisa"?

Bond: It's bigger. And it's got more colours in it.

Judge: Mr Bond, I wonder if I could ask you, the entrepreneur is not cosseted from moral sensibility. I'm sure you, in any action you undertake, have a sense of what is right and what is wrong.

Bond: Your Flagship, do me a favour. Don't come the ethics and moral values. I pumped $17 million of my own money into Rothwells Bank to run a rescue mission to stabilise the bank and protect the ordinary investors.

Turnbull: Did you receive a fee for this?

Bond: For putting $17 million of my own money into a rescue operation for the benefit of thousands of small investors? Yes of course I did.

Turnbull: How much?

Bond: Sixteen million dollars.

Judge: Seems very reasonable to me.

Turnbull: [Looks up from documents.] You own a number of companies, Mr Bond.

Bond: Wrong again. I own one company. I only ever owned one company. Dalhold P/L. I still own it.

Turnbull: Surely Bond Brewing is owned by you.

Bond: No, it's owned by Bond Corp.

Turnbull: Which you own.

Bond: No, which is owned by Dalhold.

Turnbull: And who owns Dalhold?

Bond: I do. Keep up Malcolm, for Chrissake.

Turnbull: But you control Bond Corp through Dalhold.

Bond: I don't control Bond Corp. Dalhold does, but I don't.

Turnbull: And who controls Dalhold?

Bond: I do.

Turnbull: Bond Corp has earned income?

Bond: Historically, yes.

Turnbull: That income has been distributed to you?

Bond: That income has been distributed to Dalhold, the owner of Bond Corp.

Turnbull: And Bond Corp has more latterly sustained losses.

[Bond seems uneasy.] Bond Corp has sustained losses, Mr Bond?

Judge: Are you concerned about breaching a confidence, Mr Bond?

Bond: I regret to say Bond Corp's accumulated losses are such that the company may be placed in liquidation by its creditors.

Turnbull: The losses will be achieved by your . . . by Bond Corp's creditors?

Bond: Are you suggesting they should be achieved by Dalhold? They're Bond Corp losses. You can't hold Dalhold responsible just because the Board of Bond Corp is incapable of running a company profitably.

Turnbull: And who is the Chairman of the Board of Bond Corp?

[Bond pauses, his flow interrupted.]

Judge: Would you like us to provide you with some 'think' music, Mr Bond?

Bond: [To Turnbull.] I am.

Turnbull: Have you or your companies ever been investigated by any regulatory body in respect of the practice and conduct of your business affairs?

Bond: Well the NCSCA, or the RSPCA, or someone has had a few goes at us but they've never got us to court.

Turnbull: Why not?

Bond: They've got an annual budget of $3 million. My legal expenses are $300 million a year. We get a lot of stay of proceedings decisions. Our health isn't too good during the week.

Turnbull: Mr Bond, you have conducted business in this country which has increased the national debt beyond measure, you have produced absolutely nothing whatever, you've run the profits off-shore and charged all your expenses to the Australian taxpayer and you are currently in debt to an extent that defies description. You're one of the least successful businessmen in the history of commerce.

Bond: I'm not a businessman, Malcolm. I'm an entrepreneur.

Turnbull: What happened to all the things you told us you'd bought? The hotels and the TV and the Brewery. What happened to the America's Cup?

Bond: Went back to America.

Turnbull: What happened to Van Gogh's "Irises"?

Bond: Went back to Sothebys.

Turnbull: What happened to Channel 9?

Bond: Went back to Kerry Packer.

Turnbull: Thank you, Mr Bond. And what happened to the money?

Bond: Held in sacred trust for the shareholders.

Judge: Your much publicised success is a furphy, Mr Bond. You are free to go. [A policeman enters and approaches.]

Bond: Of course I am.

Judge: With this policeman to Court 2, where you'll find your presence is required.

Bond: [Becomes bellicose and struggles, calling to the court as he is led away] You'll never work in this town again. I demand the right to make a phone call.

[A new Treasury official arrives simultaneously and enters the box, takes the oath and prepares himself.]

Turnbull: Mr Trouser, you are with the Federal Treasury?

Judge: What is his position. Mr Turnbull? We're having some trouble working out who we're talking to.

Trouser: I'm with the Planning and Projections Department.

Judge: Are you the Head of the Treasury?

Trouser: No. I run the Planning and Projections Department.

Judge: What is it that you plan and project, Mr Trouser?

Trouser: Information comes to us as raw data from all sectors of the economy. Over a period of three months this data is analysed by our department. [Holds up several New York-phone-directory-sized books] These are the current figures. We identify trends and extrapolate them into the future and advise the government on management of the economy.

Judge: And so you are therefore responsible for the management of the economy?

Trouser: Not always, no.

Turnbull: Why not? You've analysed the figures, you've made your projections, you've extrapolated. Does the government not accept your advice?

Trouser: The government has to take into account political considerations.

Turnbull: Such as what?

Trouser: Such as how the electorate might react, what the party might want, how to sell it to caucus and whether the economic and finance ministers have got the numbers in cabinet.

Judge: Mr Turnbull, we don't want to talk to this man. We want the person who makes the decisions.

Turnbull: Who takes responsibility for these political considerations?

Trouser: Ultimately they'd be a matter for the Prime Minister.

Judge: Clerk, have the Prime Minister served with a subpoena to attend this Inquiry and give evidence.

Clerk: The Prime Minister?

Judge: Yes.

Clerk: Of Australia?

Judge: Ideally, yes.

Clerk: Do you think he'll come?

Judge: It's not an invitation, it's a subpoena. You don't RSVP to them, you turn up or you get popped in the sneezer. If he's worried about who's got more power in this country, the Prime Minister or a ceremonial official appointed by the Queen, refer him to his diary for 1975. Go ahead, Mr Turnbull.

Turnbull: Mr Trouser, you've told us that over a three-month period you collect information and analyse it for trends. What do you do when you find one?

Judge: He extrapolates.

Turnbull: So what's going to happen, Mr Trouser? In the next few months, what's a likely next development in the economy?

Trouser: I've no idea. I don't have the current information.

Turnbull: I thought this [holds up sheaf] was the current information.

Trouser: They are the current figures but they're not based on the current information.

Turnbull: The current figures are not based on current information?

Trouser: No. The current information is coming in NOW.

Turnbull: So what are the current figures based on?

Trouser: They're based on the information available at the time the current figures were being prepared

Turnbull: Which was when?

Trouser: Three months ago. The figures take three months to assemble.

Turnbull: Is it possible for you to tell what's happening now?

Trouser: Yes, of course it is.

Turnbull: When could you do that?

Trouser: In three months.

Judge: What we mean, Mr Trouser, is what is happening out there now? How are ordinary people doing? Mr and Mrs Wheelbarrow going to the supermarket, how are they coping?

Trouser: That would be the CPI Your Honour. Down two per cent.

Turnbull: That's the current figure?

Trouser: Yes. Announced this morning.

Judge: Yes, but does it describe what's happening NOW?

Trouser: We would hope so. It's the current figure.

Turnbull: For what period?

Trouser: For the current period.

Turnbull: Which ended when?

Trouser: Three months ago.

Turnbull: Do you know ANYTHING about what's happening now?

Trouser: We know what's happening currently.

Turnbull: That's three months ago. Do you know what's happening today?

Trouser: No, but I will in three months.

Judge: Do you know what happened yesterday?

Trouser: Oh come on, Your Honour, I can't see into the future. I'm not a magician.

Judge: Mr Trouser, you're going to be on your own for a bit. You'll find the accommodation fairly simple and unpretentious but you'll have plenty of time to think.

[A policeman arrives and escorts Trouser from the court.]

Judge: When you come out I want you to tell me how long I sentenced you to. I'll give you a clue. You'll be out NOW!

Trouser: Three months! That's a bit stiff isn't it?

Poetry

1989–1994

Poetry

For many years it was assumed that poetry came from England. Research now clearly demonstrates, however, that a great many of the world's most famous poets were actually Australians. Works by major poets have been discovered in various parts of Australia and are published here for the first time. This collection aims to put on record the wealth of imagery and ideas in Australian verse.

English is a language relatively new to Australia and obviously in a nation so young there can be no Icelandic Sagas, no Chaucer, and no Shakespeare[1]. Certain other works have been tragically lost. The great Neville Shelley of Eildon, for instance, survives only in the oral tradition[2]. Ewen Coleridge, the so-called 'Automatic Writer', left nothing whatever and Stumpy Byron VC[3] has not been included because so much of his work was written in Greece and Italy. It is virtually impossible to find anything from Brian Browning[4] or from 'Shagger' Tennyson, who refused point blank to write anything down.

In other respects, however, this is the most complete collection of Australian verse ever published.

Such an anthology would not be possible were it not for the kind assistance of the poets, their descendants or executors. I would also thank Ms Lurleen Hopcroft for her work in typing the manuscripts and for her tireless support and cheerful presence.

1. Although fragments have been found around Stratford-near-Horsham of a work beginning "Would there be any point in my drawing some sort of comparison between yourself and an absolute scorcher?"
2. 'Pommymandius' can still be heard in pubs but no authentic manuscript exists.
3. Stumpy Byron VC. Best known for swimming at night across the shark-infested Dardanelles in order to light fires on unoccupied beaches and confuse the Turks. The Victoria Cross was awarded posthumously since Stumpy caught the flu and died a few weeks later.
4. Brian Browning; poet and cricket-lover. Rumoured to have seen every test match played in Australia between 1922 and 1939. Best known for the work beginning "Oh to be in April now that England's here".

Anon.

Trad. (From the Harleian-Davidson MSS, British Museum. Fragment originally found during excavations for the construction of Botany Bay Gaol, 1788.)

TIDE IS IGOIN OUTE

Tide is igoin oute
Lhude yelleth yikes
Water disappeareth fast
Ebbeth before eyen
Moon it pulleth tide oute
Layeth boate on keel
Sand it stretcheth meny myle
Gulle it drifts on wynde
Season goeth round each yeare
Wind it winnow croppe
Farmer reapeth harveste fulle
Meade it fylleth cup
Polly putte ye kyttle on
We wylle all haue tea
Leaf growe sere and branch growe bare
Trees istandin bleak in field
Flocks do fall to rest in fold
Storm it beats on sturdy thatch
Snowe in isolated places
Above aboute ten thousande feet
Rains ifallin on new seed
Springeth up from groun
Mare growe heavy, cowe have calf
Lambe it poppeth oute in field
Birds isingin, suns ishinin
Fysshe ajumpin, cotton hyghe,
Nature goeth on and on
Boreth britches off

Bob Herrick

A Boer War veteran who passed away some years back, Bob is well remembered by local church people in the area where he lived and worked.

UPON JULIA'S SPEEDOS

Whenas in Speedos Julia goes,
Their fabric seemeth to expose
The wonders it doth juxtapose!
Next, when I cast mine eyes and see,
That lycra stretching each way free,
Tumescence overtaketh me!

Gavin Milton

Gavin became a political activist at university and wrote an unbroken string of pearlers: "Addidas", about a promising mate of his who threw a seven during a boat trip; "Il Ponderosa", about a group of ageing baritones trying to run a farm; and "Lost and Found", about a retirement village.

ON HIS GOVERNMENT

When I consider how my tax is spent,
And bear in mind I'm talking forty years,
Perhaps sometimes a whisker in arrears,
But by and large as incomes go, it went.
I understand the cost of unemployment,
And writing off the loans to racketeers,
I know because recession perseveres,
The rich need subsid . . . I'm sorry, adjustments,
But would you mind please, not Italian suits.
Could unconcern be slightly less baroque?
And might the crappier aspects of the play
Be slightly less accompanied by lutes?
And perhaps some footnotes might explain the joke
When the government gives Telecom away.

Rabbi Burns

The son of poor farmers, Rabbi Burns became well known for poems in the regional dialect of The Mallee.

To A Howard

Wee, sleekit, cowerin, tim'rous beastie,
I know tha's probably doing thy bestie,
But the kind'st heart wuid ha' to see
Thou's nay made a fist o' the thing,
For e'en when there's nothin at a' to say
And ye'd far better tak to th' hills fo' th' day
Tha opens thy gob a' the drop o' the noo
And thou lets the wind bloo tha tongue aroon.

Och ye poor wee laddie, ye've no got the breen,
Ye've no got the sense to come oot o' the reen,
Why don't thou gi'e it awa' and gae hame,
It's no guid th' watch if ye can't tell th' tame,
There are jobs gang aplenty awa' at the farm
Afrightening birds by waving th' arms,
Ye ken they're gae keen t' employ the bold laddies
Awa' at the links where they're lookin for caddies,
If that's no to thy taste and thou's wanting a change
Thou'll try wi' th' gunnery up a the range,
Thou'll no have much truible, thou've dun it afore,
Thou's an expert for a' that; look, 'Wanted: Small Bore'.

Tim'rous Howard – silhouette by an unknown artist.

Bill Blake

The late Bill Blake, rebel, painter and engraver, was a seasonal rabbiter who only dabbled in poetry until finishing runner-up in "New Faces" with "The Book of Thel". After that, there was no holding him and many of his works are now among the most familiar in the language.

THE WORK OF HARMONY

Whose hobs are these, whose forging shape?
What metal wrought? What noble ape
With mighty arm in clamour raises
What the bellows? What the blazes?
Is it truly thee Oh Lord,
Whose alchemy transmutes the sward?
Or is the serpent active yet?
The cygnet and the leveret
Have robed in joy and innocence,
The beauty of thy congruence.

Arnold Wordsworth

Arnold Wordsworth was a plumber in Sydney during the first half of the 19th century and was responsible for much of the underground piping in Annandale and Balmain. He lived with his sister Gail and with his mate Ewen Coleridge, who shared his interest in plumbing, poetry and Gail.

LINES COMPOSED ABOUT HALFWAY
ACROSS THE PYRMONT BRIDGE

Earth has not anything to show more fair,
Soft would he be of swede, a quid unfull,
Who would willingly forgo such a view,
For lo, the sparrow breaketh of his wind
And this entire joint looks not too foul,
Stand back, for when she goes, she bloody goes.

A. Wordsworth – a contemporary etching, probably by J S Porlock.

Fifteen Bobsworth Longfellow

Fifteen Bobsworth Longfellow was an Adelaide academic who wrote instructions for kitset model products, mainly balsa wood aircraft and submarines that ran on baking powder. The manual included here was for the assembling of a 25-foot aircraft carrier marketed by Myer stores between 1954 and 1960.

MYER'S WHOPPER

Take the pieces from the package,
Lay them out as per the graph,
Gathering the bits you'll need,
Removing what you shouldn't have.
With the implement provided
Ease the bearings to the left,
Push the little angled mullion
Up into the socket 'F'.
This will free the moulded bracket
Holding back the nylon strand,
Draw the slippery hoop and coupling
Through the right-hand rubberband.
Put the topside brown side outside,
Push the inside upside down,
Underneath the left-hand wingnut,
Press the folding backward crown.
Overlapping lifting side-flaps
Lower in to fit the screws,
Pack up tools, retire to distance,
Don protective hat, light fuse.

Ted Lear

Ted Lear popularised limericks in his A Book of Rubbish, although tragically he failed to recognise that the way to make them work was to have a filthy last line.

LIMERICKS

There was an old man with a beard,
A funny old man with a beard,
He had a big beard,
A great big old beard,
That amusing old man with a beard.

There once was a woman whose hat,
Was a regular brute of a hat,
Oh a hat she did wear,
On the top of her hair,
And everyone said "Look! A hat!"

There was an old fellow from Bong,
Who hailed in the first place from Bong,
From Bong did he come,
With Bongolian rum,
That humorous old fellow from Bong.

There was an old man with a bird,
Who was an old man with a bird,
The bird with the man,
Confessed "It's absurd,
I'm the bird with the man with the bird!"

There was an old man with a goat,
An amusing old man with a goat,
The man with the goat,
Was a man with a goat,
That interesting old man with a goat.

Emmy-Lou Dickinson

Film devotees will remember Emmy-Lou as an extra in "Witness" (directed by fellow Australian Peter Weir) but it is as a poet that she is best known to date. A very quiet person, she lives alone near Lakes Entrance and speaks only to small children on her mother's side.

Are you anybody? I'm not either,
Come over here before somebody finds us,
We'll hide so everyone fails to notice
That nobody knows where we are.

Imagine being someone, Yikes!
How appalling–like a toad–
Puffing up one's throat all day
For a lot of other warts.

* * *

Exhilaration is the coming
Of the mariner uphill,
Through the wood–along the ridge–
To the utmost peak–

From the land as if for the first time
The sailor watches the storm
With the godlike perspective
Afforded by the recognition
Of form.

* * *

What is? Is this?
Can this be? If not this–
Then what? Something else?
Nothing?
Death perhaps?

Death is not nothing–
Death is something–it happens–
It follows something else–
Or nothing–
Or something other than either–
Possibly this.

* * *

Preciousness is the essential aspect
Of all the things that are precious;
I'm pretty sure this is right–
It is certainly a lovely idea.

* * *

To wither away of boredom
With only the bee to consider
Is my choice–my right–my life–
My start–my end–my God.

* * *

I fear the small–
The slight–the brief–
The large I can deal with–
But the speck–the infinity
Inside the merest particle–
Is enormous.

Thomas the Tank Hardy

A member of the prominent Hardy family, which included Mary, Frank, James and Laurelin, Tom wrote novels but everyone agreed they were no good and he turned to poetry. The everyone who agreed his novels were no good wore their underpants on their head and could count to four.

THE FAILED BUSINESSMAN

Why Harry, my boy, and how do you do?
How lovely to see you, so prosperous too,
How came you by raiment of such quality?
"Oh hadn't you heard? I went bankrupt," said he.

The last time I saw you, you hadn't two bob.
You petitioned my brother to give you a job.
And yet now you move in high so-ci-e-ty.
"One meets a broad circle, when bankrupt," said he.

Your card here gives your address as the suite
In the bank building up at the top of the street.
You advise them, it says. And you charge them a fee?
"Yes, they're not yet aware that they're bankrupt," said he.

I must say I'm slightly surprised by your car,
The phone not so much but the TV and bar,
In times of distress, tell me how can that be?
"It belongs to my wife. She's not bankrupt," said he.

And whose are these paintings here stuffed in the back?
They must be worth millions, my God there's a stack
Of western art's finest old masters I see.
"One's pleasures are simple, when bankrupt," said he.

But surely you're working to clear all your debt,
With a management plan and advisors to get
A repayment arrangement in place so you're free.
"Oh we don't do accounts when we're bankrupt," said he.

But the company has assets and so has the trust,
Transfer them and sell them and pay what you must,
As director you must have the authority.
"Oh I wouldn't trust me. I'm a bankrupt," said he.

But your reputation will carry the stain,
You must fight to clear at all costs your good name,
We each have a right to our own dignity.
"Oh we don't give a fuck when we're bankrupt," said he.

Walter Burley Yeats

Often referred to as the authentic voice of Tasmania, Walter Burley Yeats was elected Senator in 1922, and won the Nobel Prize for Shearing in 1931, 1932 and 1933.

THE FLASHING GYRE

I run with the old men, piping their song,
The moon-mad and troubled engaged in a reel,
The careless white hair of them streaming along,
As they dance in the tops of the trees,
The loopy old men, the wild-eyed and punching,
Who better than know their heart's beat?
For old men know of old women,
And old women have dreams at their feet.
I mistook the quickening fiddler's hand
For the swan-beat of wings passing by,
For old men are merry when roaring with fire,
And birds and old women lament with the sky.
Or why if the wandering wind-dried MacCool
And Brigid hold hands at the Hobart Fair
Should not old men salmon-leap into the ditch,
Remembering glances that sang on the air?

Arthur 'Guitar Boogie' Patterson

You can smell gum trees in the nation's authentic verse, full of bush lore and traditional yarns, many slightly exaggerated in a typically larrikin way but with a strong and distinctive rhythm, which seems to come from deep among the mountain wattles and is unlike any other verse in the English language.

THE AUTHENTIC AUSTRALIAN BUSH BALLAD

There was kipling at the Kipling for the kipling got around,
That the colt they called 'The Kipling' got away.
It was worth a thousand kiplings and it vanished overnight,
And it took off up the Rudyard where the kiplings often go.

So the kiplings came from everywhere preparing for the fray,
Every man who'd ever kippled, every man who knew the way,
Glinting sunlight caught the bridle of the youngest man among them
He was rather like a kipling under-sized.

But the shout that spurred them onward lifted hands and heels together
And they kippled up the Rudyard with their eyes upon the prize,
No one ever saw such kipling, ne'er were man and horse together
Nor as swift nor sure-footed as they climbed.

But the mob was kipling faster and was down the other side
And heading straight toward the Rudyard where they knew that they could hide.
And the old man wheeled and halted, standing kipling at the prospect
That his colt was gone beyond where even mountain man could ride.

And he knew, all hope receding, no one now could head the mob,
For never yet were horse and rider seen,
Who could follow once the brumbies made the treeline up the Rudyard
Kipling wild and kipling free in places man has never been.

Then a roar was heard of horses crashing through the rocks and tundra,
And the old man's fingers tightened on the rein,
For any mob that crossed the river made the toughest alpine scrub,
That ever mountain soil could sustain.

But a new sound filled the valley as the brumbies broke their cover
And across the river tracings ran for home,
And the old man turned to Clancy and he thought he caught him smiling
When he asked him who could get down there alone.

And again the snap of whipcrack and the men could see the pack
With now a single rider gaining from the rear.
And they could hear the young man yelling, how he'd got there, no one knew,
Clancy said that he'd be buggered and he promised him a beer.

And they watched with hearts akippling for their spirits now were lifting
And they stood up in their stirrups and they cheered.
Riding flank to flank they saw him, with the fastest of the mob,
If they made the other bank the lot were gone.

But he headed them and held them and the leaders turned and halted.
They were beaten and they knew it. They were done.
And exhausted, wet and foaming they began the journey home
In the warm softness of the steeply banking sun.

There's a green and yellow wattle to the north of Reedy Creek,
Where the air is thick with thousands of galahs,
Where the men will treat you badly but if you can turn the mob
You can tell them all to stick it up their arse.

If you're better off without them, if you'd rather be alone
If you can get off on your own just near the start,
If you're too young to be frightened and you don't know where you're going
And you don't mind if you rip your gear apart.

And if you can go down hillsides very near the speed of sound,
And manage somehow not to fall or hit a tree
Then there's every a chance some bully will extend a manly grasp,
Clear his throat and tell you "You're a man, my son."

And if you can fight the impulse to be swayed by this display
And you remember his behaviour in the past
And you can learn to shake a hand while saying "Jab it up your arse."
Then you'll find the next bit easy. Walk away.

Blank Verse

Jems Choice

Jems is one of Tasmania's best-known exports. He left Hobart with Enid Carbuncle before World War I and never went back. He got a job teaching English in Brisbane and began work on his novels. His first works were heavily criticised in the Tasmanian press and he spent the rest of his life writing one that no one would understand.

THE BALLAD OF JASPER O'REILLY

Nearly recovered we are blathered here today
In the flight-path of Himself
Dijon disbanding this woman in howdy-doodiedom
Do you (insert your trained leer, Mr Earwicker)
Take Anna Livia to be or not
To be your lawful dreaded life?
Eyedew.
Under you, Anna Livia, talk this man
(Insert your train here, Mr Wicker)
To be your awful bedded strife?
Adieu.
If anybum nose often impedimenta
Speak nowra four of a whole jaw-piece.

Unpack the voluminous dative case and lay out
The suit my grammar left me the mardi da,
The mither of the fither sun and noilly pratt
Parse the photo correction, lookit the faces,
Theres Dante, dont minchinbury legion,
Seether man in the hat? Boylan for the wife he is
Cant get enough off her always warm in the bed.

This hears Molly wither clothiers on
And thesis the dress under where just under there
The underwear sur prize sur prize
All stand while we observe the holy trinity
Come come now Mr Deedless do not toy with the caught
Put them on a good behaviour bond
Ant twatted he say when he touched you my child?
Pig in your porter butters this seat taken?
Nature of Inquiry;
Genuine, searching, passibly dooble onton,
Character of response;
Fellatious, mollified, deeply touched,
Dr Ring will free you now three cheers no waiting.

The fiddle he diddled the dada did
He middled the little La Scalas id
Belittled the riddle the fathers hid
Skedaddled and addled the sorters of
The muddle was on for supporters of
And all of the Murraying waters of
The hurry and worrying waters of
Lights going
Fights going
Sights going
All of the sons and daughters of
The trouble enchanted ought is off
For all of the martyred daughters of
Night.

R.A.C.V. Milne

Essayist, poet and commercial traveller, R.A.C.V. Milne wrote a number of verses for children. His best-known works are still read today. In the 1980s the government attempted to introduce a personal ID card for every citizen. Like many others, Milne thought only banks and secret agencies should have carefully cross-referenced data bases. He reacted immediately.

THE DOG'S BREAKFAST

Bob asked Neil,
And Neil asked Susan,
Do you think that we could rustle up support for the I.D.?
Neil spoke to Susan,
Susan said "Certainly,
I'll go about the countryside and see what I can see."

So Susan she took her leave,
And went down to Tasmania,
And told them they were ignorant
And stupid as could be,
And they didn't understand,
And the government would have its way,
The card was coming in and everybody should agree.

But the people said they didn't,
And they couldn't and they wouldn't,
And they shouldn't, it was rotten,
But that even if they did,
Who was going to have access
To the facts about the taxes?
How could anybody guarantee complete security?

So Susan went to Neil,
She told him of the news,
She told him how the people felt
And how she'd been accused
Of invading of the privacy
Attempting to dehumanise
And tamper with the sanctity of individual rights.

Susan told Neil,
And Neil went to Bob,
Bob said "Bother",
Or words to that effect,
He fulminated briefly,
Said that what he wanted chiefly
Was to do the thing for which
He'd asked the people to elect him.

But John put the card to sleep,
Establishing his fame,
And great was the rejoicing
Of the folk who thought the same,
But we're left with the position
That in keeping with tradition
It's the rich to which the pleasure
And the poor to whom the blame.

OBVIOUSNESS

Rob Rob Bobbity Bobbity James Lee Hawke M.P.
Took great care of his image because he was quick to see
That if you are photographed standing with blokes
Whose boats do well on the sea,
Millions of voters will fail to notice
The blokes will be charging a fee.

(This couldn't happen in New Zealand.)

William Esther Williams

Williams was a doctor whose interest in Imagist poetry helped him greatly in his work. Very interested in nature, especially, like Marianne More, in the pantheistic resonance of great big animals.

THE CARNIVAL

Why is it that every year
On remote coastlines
Labour leaders
Beach themselves?
Whole schools of them,
Apparently healthy Labour leaders
Thousands of miles off course and stranded,
Spume drifting from their tragic holes.

Why do they do it?
Is it not knowing where they are going?
Or is it guilt over where they have been?
There is no more futile prospect in nature
Than ordinary folk with flippers and buckets
Working urgently in the deepness of the shore
To turn the stricken Labour leaders around
Before nightfall.

Kahlihliji Bran

Kahlihliji was a migrant to Australia, settling in Sydney from Lebanon. He had studied sculpture under Rodin but at that time nobody in Australia had heard of either Rodin or sculpture. Kahlihliji became a visionary.

THE HALF-YEARLY PROPHET

And a Punter came forth, which was not unusual, and said
Speak to us of Race 5 at Randwick.
And he answered and said:
Goodness me, is that the time?
People of Moron, I say to you, Wisdom is not in others. It is
in ourselves. We are not others. Other people are. We
are us. And yet they are not Them. They are merely an Us
which does not include anyone here. Any questions so far?
The world is a seamless cloth. Take shelter in it but do not
expect it to fit.
Love and Understanding are but winds that bear the spirit.
Love may be given but cannot be taken.
Understanding can be neither given nor taken but is the
string in the bow of Life.
We are not Us either, incidentally, I should make this
clear. Just a small one thanks.
Everything is its own opposite.
Paradox is that which is not paradoxical.
Only the living know death. Only the dead are living.
Only the lonely, dum dum dum dumdedoowah, know the
way I feel tonight. Jameson's if they've got it.
A cow has many windows, but only one rudder.
Reason is a tool. Try to remember where you left it.
If you are rich and you would give, give not your money.
The poor know nought of money. Give them of yourself.
A smile, a pat on the head, something of that order.
And he beckoned to the pilot.
I must take rest for a time, he said, possibly on Venus.
And he was gone.

Alain Frost

Frost, three-time winner of the Zitpuller Prize, holds a venerable position in world letters, partly because of his great age. He was at one time the oldest white male poet writing in English. Sadly, 86 years later, he died.

THE TRACK LESS THRASHED

Two tracks leading nowhere in the bush
Miles from anywhere, I rolled the window
Down and had a look up the first one,
Considered the position briefly and
Said I preferred the other one. My father
Looked up from his form guide and asked me why,
I said because it's not this one. You talk
To him mother, he said, I cannot deal
With him, the boy's a bloody idiot.
There's no need for language, said my mother.

While the matter was discussed I climbed
A very large redgum out over the river
And in a sense I never quite came down.
The great thing about being up a tree
Is that you're not going along a track.

T.S. (Tabby Serious) Eliot

Tabby Serious Eliot was born in Mallacoota but went to school and university in Melbourne, qualifying as a surveyor in 1915. Among his other works is Old Ponce's Book of Practical Webbers.

THE ACCOUNTING CAT

Liquidity's a mystery; it's very rarely seen,
It strikes and then is gone again, its getaway is clean,
And despite forensic evidence and great deductive flair,
The conclusion's inescapable, Liquidity's not there!

Liquidity, Liquidity, there's nothing like Liquidity,
Its presence gives you confidence, its absence is timidity,
You own perhaps a property, you own perhaps a share,
But once you've lost your credit card, Liquidity's not there!
Your understated opulence inheres in what you wear,
But in the end you face the fact, Liquidity's not there!

Liquidity's a nifty term, it's business talk for cash,
It's money not tied up in things or hoovered in the crash,
Investments may return amounts of staggering obscenity,
The vastness of your holdings may explain your great serenity.
In publishing, to take the case of either of the Fabers,
A warehouse full of Larkin and The Bumper Book of Neighbours,
Is very well, and when they sell, will satisfy the editors,
But not much use, in real terms, when dealing with the creditors.

Liquidity, Liquidity, there's nothing like Liquidity,
The glint of actual ducats brings respect and dipthelidity,
It's likely to self-immolate on contact with the air,
Say "Raffle" in a crowded room; Liquidity's not there!

In the conduct of a company (proprietary limited),
There's always a suspicion that the system's maladministered,
In proper corporate planning you allow a little spare,
But when you need the wherewithal, Liquidity's not there!

Liquidity, Liquidity, there's nothing like Liquidity,
In purely economic terms it constitutes validity,
I wish I had a pound for every credit millionaire,
Who completely failed to register, LIQUIDITY WASN'T THERE!
When reputations tumble and the search is on for clues,
(I might mention humpo-bumpo, I might mention drinkie-poos)
There's a suspect who can prove he was in Lima at the time,
They can't catch him, he's the brilliant Scarlet Pimpernel of crime!

THE LOVE SONG OF J. ARTHUR PERPEND

Let us go then, you and I,
While there's still time to read and classify,
Measuring the margins on the little fey barometer
That marks the calibrations of our talk.

In the room the women come and go
Despite what I read in the papers.

Old is what I seem increasingly to be,
Tobacco-tranced in time I watch the sea,
It was a dark and stormy old pyjama cord
That lashed me to my dream of others moored,
There followed soft a moment put on hold
With a wind without a rug against the cold
And someone, call it someone, up on an elbow,
For argument's sake, might say,
"You have missed the point,
You have completely missed the point."

In the room the women come and go
But not, perhaps regrettably, with me.

Marianne More

Born near Broken Hill, Marianne More has always had a feeling for the expanse and majesty of Australia and the natural world. She went to school in Adelaide.

THE MAJESTY OF GREAT BIG ANIMALS

The majesty of bison as they roam,
Is awesome, in the North, in spring, I've seen,
The majesty of lizards, and observed,
The majesty of easy climbing birds,
Whose majesty is manifest in groups.

The trees are in their awesome beauty now,
Majestic kangaroos abound in scores,
And groups of birds lift lazily and wheel,
Like lazy groups of wheeling birds aloft,
Especially near a river, did you ever
Just consider, the majesty of rivers?

Dorothy Parkinson

Writer of bittersweet reviews and short stories. Member of the famous Algongwoin 'Drunks' group.

THE STORY SO FAR

Poland works nicely,
Chad's going well,
Burma's precisely
Successful as hell,
Haiti is lovely,
This time of year,
Sudan is just darling,
Thank God for Zaire,
Chile's a dish,
Brazil is a dream,
South Africa's bliss,
And Iran is a scream.
Go lease a car,
Go purchase a suit,
Everything's ducky,
And I'm King Canute.

b.b. hummings

b.b. drove an ambulance in World War I and was mistakenly imprisoned by the French. He never fully recovered and returned to Australia in some confusion. Tragically, he did not know he wrote poetry. He thought it was "just a lot of nonsense".

74

this bit

foll
owe
db
y

this bit

and

                              then

                                                      this bit
                                                      over here

                                              n
seasons change and leaves go   w
                              u   o
                          p   d
                          o r

coolman;unmanuncool
(nothing)

?

huh?

Ogden Gnash

Ogden Gnash was perhaps the best known of the Perth poets.

PARDON ME MADAM BUT IS THAT MANDIBLE ON A LEASH OR WHAT?

Of all the tenets mentioned in discussions about levity,
By far the most important and the best of them is brevity,
So Shakespeare and Railway Timetables and instruction
   manuals in foreign languages apart,
Be, of all literary forms, most suspicious of the poem which
   is almost entirely parenthetical and despite whose
   Towards More Picturesque Speech homely
   cleverness in the Norman Rockwell manner, leaves
   you wondering whether you've left the gas on and
   whether you've got to throw another six to start.

W.H. Auding

Wisty Huge Auding published his first collection, Poems, in 1928, followed by A Whole Lot More in 1932 and When We Were Very Old in 1960. He died in 1968, 1971, and again in 1973.

MUSE OF BAUXITE

About Telecom they were never wrong,
The Old Masters, how prescient they were
About existential services;
How well they knew the mundane brutality of increasing
charges for items which don't exist,
How, while oafs deliberate, holding money
Up to the light, agreeing it should be described
Not as a profit but as an operating surplus,
There always must be, bleak-faced, random and frantic,
Victims, trying to make urgent calls on public phones dangling
From walls in a twisted piss-smelling tardis,
And in the distance a man sits on a park-bench,
Explaining to his grandchild the merits of competition.

In Nolan's Ned Kelly series, for instance, how everyone's face
Is either hidden or green; hidden, encased
In metal, in uniform, angled, straight and hard,
Or green, and how, when Scanlon is shot from his horse
And falls, he falls up,
Unsurprised, a bystander,
He's thinking "Dearie me,
Another balls-up."

Louis 'The Lip' MacNeice

Recruited from Northern Tasmania in 1925, MacNeice became one of the mainstays of Australian verse between the wars.

WHAT I DID IN THE HOLIDAYS

Section IX
In a week I shall return to the University
And begin again the selection of anecdotes,
Revealing the ageless to the briefly young,
Explaining the dead to the living,
Arranging the facts in a circle and playing
Simon says The Glory of Greece.
Balance your chair on the bookcase,
Study the dust in a shaft of light,
And listen to the familiar stories,
Nod with the names, salute the heroes,
The paragons, the exceptions that prove the rules;
Plato, Diogenes, Alcibiades,
The Thracian vases, Delphi on a clear day,
Liking the Spartans less because we
Could never do that with our young.
Observe the neat morals, the perfect natural laws,
The foundations of modern justice:
At least one foot must be on the floor
While towing Hector around the walls of Troy.
Gentlemen are requested to wear a jacket
During the putting out of eyes,
Lotuses should not be consumed in the upstairs bedrooms,
Persons tied to rocks and women with uncontrollable boxes
May be charged accordingly.
A code not so much to be used as admired,
To know the classical, the ordered, the decent,
From the random pillage of the horde,
And to decide whether I am part of the one

Or simply at odds with the other,
And to pick at the seam of this discipline,
Which presents the apotheosis as the norm,
Which dresses the writers, the dramatists,
The hypocrites, the philosophers and the lads
Who drew right-angles in the sand with sticks,
As the standard, the usual things
Done in the usual way.

And I think myself of the blockheads, the pimps,
The hired thugs and the imposters,
The mountebanks with imported sandals,
And the developer's brother-in-law
Who spoke in the Agora securing the right
To flatten some olive groves mentioned in Hesiod
And open a π shop.

FLAGPOLE MUSIC

It's no go the tight-head prop, it's no go the hooker,
Wait till the bloody thing's put in straight and review it for *The New Yorker*,
Wystan Hugh went up to Iceland in a shower of rain,
Addressed an epistle as Juan's apostle and buggered a dog on a chain,

It's no go the Willie Away, it's no go the droppie,
Run it and draw the defence in the centre and stick up a kick if it's sloppy,

Oliver Gogarty went for a swim and put in a personal best,
Presented the Liffey with plenty of swans and did what he could for the rest,
The appendectification of Yeats, the Celtification of John,
The Mulliganising of Martello Jim, the Newdigate Prize having gone,

It's no go the halftime score, it's no go relaxing,
They'll come out of there like a bull at a gate after getting a boot in the jacksie,

Roger Casement looking to drive, splitting the men in the covers,
Caught in the lovely Republic of Irony, strung up as high as his lovers,
Bernard Shaw went to visit himself, sequestered away in a castle,
And F. E. Smith, should it please the court, fellated the late King's arsehole,

And it's no go *Hotel ∂u Lac*, it's no go the Amis,
The Booker is rigged and boring as shit and the publishers want to be famous,

It's no go the final effort, it's no go the gumption,
It's into the showers and out of the steam and off to the after-match function,

It's no go the Wittgenstein, it's no go linguistics,
It's no go the sober pricks, quickly becoming the pissed-pricks,
It's no go the Cabaret, it's no go the ball gown,
All we want is a bang in the dark and a mate and bottle of fall down,
It's no go the juxtapose, it's no go the finger,
Ladies and gentlemen join with me now in formally thanking the singer.

Dylan Thompson

Martyr to the turps, Dylan Thompson frequently woke in unfamiliar circumstances and attempted to catch the speech rhythms of the sea.

A Child's Christmas In Warrnambool

One Christmas was so like another in those years around
the sea town corner now, that I can never remember
whether it was 106 degrees in 1953 or whether it was 103
degrees in 1956. All the Christmases roll into one down
the wave-roaring salt-squinting years of yesterboy.
My hand goes into the fridge of imperishable memory and out
come: salads and sunburn lotions, the brief exuberant hiss
of beer being opened and the laugh of wet-haired youths
around a Zephyr 6, the smell of insect repellent and
eucalyptus and the distant constant slowly listless bang of
the flywire door. And resting on a formica altar, waiting
for Ron, the biggest Pav in the world; a magic Pav,
a cut-and-come-again Pav for all the children in all the towns
across the wide brown bee-humming trout-fit sheep-rich
two-horse country.
And the Aunts. Always the Aunts. In the kitchen on the
black-and-white photographed beach of the past, playing
out the rope to a shared childhood, caught in the
undertow and drifting.
And some numerous Uncles, wondering sometimes why they weren't
each other, coming around the letterbox to an attacking
field in the Test match and being driven handsomely by
some middle-order nephew, skipping down the vowel-
flattening pitch and putting the ball into the tent-flaps on
the first bounce of puberty.

Anne Bonkford

Bonkford studied with Robert Bowell and wasn't mad either. At all. Her concerns are those of the self in daily life, particularly that of the east coast beaches.

Where Was JFK When He Heard That I Was Shot?

One morning in 1962, a beautiful woman, husky-voiced,
Married but not completely satisfied within three months
Fell in love with God in the supermarket
While she was looking at some sunglasses.
He was the one, she knew. That face.
Those eyes. This was it. She was gone.
She would have given her life for him.

"Who are you," she asked.
"I am Yahweh," he said.
"What do you do?" she said.
"I am a creator," he said.
"A creator?" she said, "Really?
I've never seen you at the meetings."
"I am everywhere," he said.
"I am a bit all over the place myself," she said.
"I am the light and the way," he said.
"I'll bet you are," she said. "Is there a Mrs Yahweh?"
"No," he said with a smile which surpassed all understanding.
"You're single?" she asked.
"No," he answered, "I am three."
"I understand," she said, "I'm in exactly the same position."

Derek Benaud

Man of the Series at the 1992 World Literature Awards. His work reflects a deep concern for his country's uncertain future and captures beautifully the rhythm of the local patois and the prospect of perhaps a light shower later in the day.

THE CENTRAL COMMENTARY POSITION

The devil is coming in off the long run
And I am batting. Last man in and four hundred years to win back
The first one going down leg side I stand up
And pull it round the corner, get on to it nicely
And loft it into the number three stand. The crowd goes mad.
The devil is coming down the pitch with the hands
On the hips, looking at me with the stare, the evil stare.
The next one straight at my head, I lean away and flick it
Over the slips cordon to the boundary. This time he's really angry.
He's a red man now the devil. Is there a Mrs Devil I wonder,
Does she have to put up with this sort of crap every time
She expresses herself?
All right for him but a different rule for the natives.
That's the way. I bet that's the way.
That's the way it always works, well come on Mr Devil,
Let's see what you've got, and the next one looking to york me but
I come down the wicket and make a full toss of it and he watches
It go over his head and into the sightscreen and the crowd is
Dancing and banging the lids together and laughing and the man
At the non-striker's end is coming down and talking to me.
Calm down he says, don't be too hot-headed, this man, he's good.
Good? I say. He's no good. He's bad.
This is rubbish he's bowling. We can take him apart.
Better not, he says, prodding the pitch
With the toe of his Stuart Surridge.
Why not? I say.
He buys eighty-seven per cent of our sugar, he says.
The ball is there to be hit, I say
As drinks come on to the ground
And we return you now to the studio.

Sylvia Blath

Born in Mosman, Sylvia wrote about illness and death. She sometimes did it ironically but always, behind all the fun, were illness and death. She called it a day in 1963.

SELF DEFENCE

You do no soft, you do no soft,
No more the old soft shoe,
In which I once delighted when you
Danced upon my cradle, as I
Annexed the Sedatenland.

I clapped my partly German hand,
On my partly Polish one,
Just like in real life,
And when you came home, achtung!
You wiped your boots on my face.

In the shadows you ordered away the lives
Of all of us black Jewish Poles,
Your daughter you condemned
To the oven, subtle in leather,
Der Ofen! Schnell!

Pig brute fatso bastard,
Shit bugger bum fuck poos,
Daddy Daddy I'm through, Hello?
Germaine I can hardly hear you,
This is a very bad line.

Nob Dylan

Nob came originally from Charade, a small town near Piffle, NSW. His real name was Ern Zimmermalley and his work turned out to have been an elaborate joke concocted by other poets, notably James Dean and Woody Guthrie.

RAIN PAIN TRAIN SONG NUMBER 407B

Lyric reprinted from The Genius of Nob Dylan by Nob Dylan. By kind permission of the publishers, Zimmerdrivel Productions.

There's a martyr standing laughing on the dark side of the road
There's a crimson coloured fire across the land
And Iscariots in every house hold tightly to their dream
With their thirty silver reasons in their hand
Their graven image worshipping their horn of stolen plenty
Singing songs that make the river want to cry

Give me that old time religion
That old time religion
Give me that old time religion
I'm as radical as a chocolate frog
Give me that old time religion
That old time religion
Give me that old time religion
You've got to do as you're told by someone
And it might as well be me

The Mississippi moon comes up the window of the train
Making good time down to Frisco in the early morning rain
I can't get me no interest rates, Oh Lord, I can't, oh no
I can't get me no short term market, Oh Lord, I can't, no mo'
Ain't no one prepared to pay twenty, Great Jesus, you tell me
Please tell me how's a workin man spose to live
Give me that old time religion
That old time religion

Give me that old time religion
I'm as radical as a chocolate frog
Give me that old time religion
That old time religion
Give me that old time religion
You've got to do as you're told by someone
And it might as well be me

We got a call at work today from some guy on the road,
Crosses shifted, any distance, family business, nothing down,
Smart kid wanted with own transport, who must know at least
Three ways, of getting out to Calvary from town
And a man with bleeding feet came in to shelter from the storm,
And he said he'd take it right away but he wanted Mondays off

Give me that old time religion
That old time religion
Give me that old time religion
I'm as radical as a chocolate frog
Give me that old time religion
That old time religion
Give me that old time religion
You've got to do as you're told by someone
And it might as well be me

Leonard Con

A deeply sensitive and wickedly humorous writer whose use of irony is greatly admired by very small children.

THE EMPEROR'S NEW ALBUM

I want you but I don't deserve you
My soul is not healthy or clean
For a moose with undisciplined trousers
Is slightly less smart than it seems

But you'd like my friend, his name's Jesus
He's tall and he's handsome and cool
He's especially relaxed among lepers
He's the grooviest kid in the school

I awake from a dream that I'm sleeping
In the soft magazine of your hair
It's warm and it's dark and it's raining
And I'm coming to Scarborough Fair

There's a man on the TV who's standing
On a mountain of glasses and shoes
They've ambushed the train from Vienna
On the six and a half o'clock news

There are ten thousand Arian women
In position and firing at will
I'll take the ones in the tower
And Jesus the fools on the hill

And we synchronise watches and guide books
And our weapons, false papers and charts
General Mills on deployment of symbols
General Boon on the breaking of hearts

Then I'll send in my troops in their millions
I've trained them to swim in the dark
Resistance is futile, we're poets,
And we'll touch your perfect bodies
With our shlong

La la la la la la la la
La la la la la la la
La la la la la la la la
La la la la la la la

Margaret Attwood

Margaret comes from the bush up near Cooma and writes almost everything produced in Cooma. As well as her poetry she has produced a number of novels, mainly about Cooma.

EVERYONE DANCES

Look Janet look.

See Janet run.

Why is Janet running?

More particularly why is she running from John?

Can anyone think of a reason why she might be running towards Peter?

How many people have spotted Janet's mistake?

Janet wants to be a nurse when she grows up.
Janet wants to help people.
Janet is a people person.

Oliver wants to be a doctor and cure diseases.
Oliver is too young to know what doctors really do.

Oliver and Janet attain their majorities and meet at a party at Peter's house.
They fall in love over half a bottle of wine and a Raoul Dufy print and they leave in Oliver's powerful thrusting sports car.

Oliver turns out to be a complete arsehole of course.
How many of you noticed me setting him up?

Janet runs into John at a Woody Allen movie and,
although John is almost as boring as the Woody Allen
movie, he offers stability and reasonable genetic
stock. They marry and Janet has two babies almost
immediately.

Janet loves her children but something is missing.
After a time of wonder, she identifies the missing
element as Peter. She meets Peter at a series of
rendezvous so as not to alert Peter's wife. This works
well and John is not at all suspicious since he is not
that sort of person. He is the sort of person who has
been corking his secretary, the lissome Fiona, for
nearly four years.

Janet and Peter eventually find their affair becoming
slightly less magical so they give it away and go back
to civilian life. Peter makes a confession to his wife
in which he pretends to recognise her value and blames
himself in a manner which makes her feel responsible.

Janet drinks like a fish and St John the Martyr feels
justified in manipulating Fiona.

Can we all see the people Janet helped?

Can Janet see?

Look Janet look.

Television

Interviews

1989–1996

Interview conducted with P.J. Keating,
Treasurer of Australia. March 1989.

Mr Keating, thanks for your time.
A pleasure. Have some brie.
Can I ask if you've seen the recent figures?
The Cost of Living figures?
Yes.
Yes, they're very distressing aren't they?
You're not happy with them?
It's beginning to look as if we've made some very big mistakes. We've taken policy positions on interest rates, deregulation of the currency market and so on and, as I say, it looks as if we were wrong.
Are you saying it's not working?
It's a complete cock-up.
How did the Government misread things so badly?
It wasn't the Government; it was me. I had a pretty good run for a while there but the wheels have come off. She's cactus.
What went wrong?
I'm probably not the person to ask. I haven't known too much about what's been going on since the middle of 1985. Perhaps I should have said so earlier but when you're the Treasurer you can't go about the place revealing your own incompetence by telling people to abandon ship. It's been a hell of a thing to live with.
If I can say this without appearing insensitive, that's probably not the issue.
No, you're right. I've got to stop thinking about myself all the time. It must have been bloody terrible for a lot of people out there. How they've coped I'll never know. It says a great deal about ordinary Australians you know, this whole business. You feel helpless; all that trust and not a bloody clue about what you're doing.
If I could just take you back over some of the things the Government has done . . .
Not the Government. Let's be completely clear about this. The policies were mine. It is entirely my fault.
Can I ask you about the May Economic Statement in 1987?
Shot in the dark.
Didn't come off?
Never looked like it, unfortunately. Although, of course, the real problem last year was the Budget itself.

What aspect of it?

All of it. It actually goes back to the 1984 Budget. That's where I lost the plot and realised that, if I just let the economy run, I might be able to dress the results up as our policy; analyse things retrospectively and stress our commitment to whatever appeared to be happening.

Is this where the J Curve comes from?

Yes.

What exactly was the J Curve?

I just don't recall exactly what it was now. It might have been a reflection of the way reduced domestic demand translated into a control mechanism for lessening foreign indebtedness over time, but don't hold me to that. I'm not sure that's right.

Didn't it have something to do with money supply?

It may have. I don't know.

Is it possible for the economy to actually change direction, which is what you seem to be suggesting?

Part of the problem is that the economic advisors and analysts have all been trained by the system that has got us into this position. None of them has any knowledge of how to change it or what to change it to. All we can do is hope to develop a better sort of Elastoplast. The possibility of actual change is nil.

But isn't it needed?

It's needed urgently, yes. No doubt about that. I'm just telling you it isn't going to happen.

What do you think are the main problems at the moment?

Oh Christ, where to start. Interest rates are appalling, people can't afford to buy houses, we're committed to unemployment, we've trimmed public expenditure so much the place doesn't work, and if the Japanese stop investing in Australia for five minutes it's all over.

Why don't you lower interest rates?

We can't afford to; we're pretending to give tax cuts and that's where we're getting the money from.

Why did you make a speech recently blaming people who live in houses with Hill's Hoists and so on?

I haven't been well. I seem to recall giving it a bit of a nudge before making those remarks. It's pointless blaming the victims, of course, and I deeply regret any offence I may have given.

Do you have any concern about the type of society you're creating here?

Yes, that is very worrying. A lot of cowboys have got the run of the joint at the moment. If you saw some of the mongrels I have to deal with your hair would stand bolt upright.

How have your colleagues reacted to the news?

By and large very well. I've had a lot of support; not from everyone but that's understandable. There were plenty of people in the Government who disagreed with me from day one.

Who were they?

Oh, Barry Jones and all those brainy pricks.

But weren't they right?

Yes, but I didn't know that then. I thought I had a dream. I didn't know it was just a lot of ego until it was too late.

What will you do?

I'll stay in the job because I've told Bob I would, but I don't know how long I can go on pretending.

You feel you've let the country down?

Of course. I've let the country down very badly. Tell the people I am deeply, deeply, deeply sorry.

I will.

Interview with a Spokesman for BHP.

Thanks for joining us.
Pleasure.
You're having a dispute with Greenpeace over your exploration off the coast.
Well, there is some ground between us left to cover. The precise detail you see, of what we're doing seismically is somewhat at odds with the general principles espoused by the Greenpeace organisation; general principles, I might say, which we also espouse; general principles the espousal of which would be axiomatic, I would think, to any understanding of environmental issues.
Yes. Could you be more specific?
Yes. We were going to dig a dirty great hole in the seabed because there's a quid in it and we got caught and we're rather embarrassed about it.
What do Greenpeace say is wrong with what you're doing?
They say the area we're thinking of digging up is a whale-breeding area.
Is it?
No. It's not.
It isn't?
No. Well, that is to say, it won't be.
When won't it be?
It won't be when the whales get out of the area, will it?
Where are the whales going to go?
I don't know. I don't even know that there are any whales there.
Isn't it a breeding ground, though?
I've never seen any whales breeding out there.
Well, have you been out there?
Of course I've been out there. I was out the other day.
On a whale-spotting boat?
No, on a dirty big new drilling rig we've got that can displace an area the size of India in an hour-and-a-half. Fantastic thing.
And there were no whales breeding?
I didn't see any.
Did you hear any?
I beg your pardon?
Where are they going to breed then?
I don't know, but I can tell you something; they don't breed in the sea out there.
Where, other than the sea out there, do you think whales breed?
I don't know about whale breeding. I'm not making myself very clear. Dirty great holes in the seabed I can do for you, knowledge about whales I don't have, but I'll tell you something about your whale; he's not a moron. The whale is a very

intelligent critter. I've seen them going through hoops at Seaworld. Your whale's got enough brains to get out of the area while we're drilling, for goodness sake.

Can I put it another way? Is there oil there, under the seabed?

We don't know but we currently think so.

Have you got shares in BHP? Are you a shareholder?

Yes of course I am.

Have you got any shares in whales?

No, you can't get shares in a whale, son. You don't buy shares in whales. Horses yes, whales no. I've got a share in a horse.

How do you get a return from that?

They breed. You breed them. Why would you breed a whale? Your whale's got no speed and he can't stay; he's no good over hurdles and he's useless on the flat.

Thanks for joining us.

Have you ever backed a whale? I can't remember when I last backed a whale.

We're out of time, I'm sorry.

You'll get decent odds, son, but keep your money in your pocket.

An Interview with Senator Collins, Minster for Transport.

Senator Collins, thanks for coming in.
It's a great pleasure.
This ship that was involved in the incident off Western Australia this week . . .
The one the front fell off? That's not very typical, I'd just like to make that point.
How is it untypical?
Well, there are a lot of these ships going round the world all the time and very seldom does this happen. I just don't want people thinking that tankers aren't safe.
Was this tanker safe?
Well, I was thinking more about the other ones.
The ones that are safe?
Yes. The ones the front doesn't fall off.
If this tanker wasn't safe, why did it have 80,000 tonnes of oil in it?
I'm not saying it wasn't safe, it's just perhaps not as safe as some of the other ones.
Why?
Well some of them are built so that the front doesn't fall off at all.
Was this one built so that the front didn't fall off?
Obviously not.
How do you know?
Because the front fell off and 20,000 tonnes of crude oil spilt out and the sea caught fire. It's a bit of a giveaway. I'd just like to make the point that that is not normal.
What sort of standards are they built to, these oil tankers?
Oh, very vigorous maritime engineering standards.
What sort of thing?
Well, the front's not supposed to fall off for a start.
And what other things?
There are regulations governing the materials they can be made of.
What materials?
Well, cardboard's out.
And?
No cardboard derivatives.
Paper?
No paper. No string, no Sellotape.
Rubber?

No, rubber's out. They've got to have to have a steering wheel. There's a minimum crew requirement.

What's the minimum crew?

Oh. One, I suppose.

So the allegation that they're just designed to carry as much oil as possible and to hell with the consequences, that's ludicrous is it?

Absolutely ludicrous. These are very very strong vessels.

So what happened in this case?

Well, the front fell off in this case by all means, but it's very unusual.

But Senator Collins, why did the front fall off?

A wave hit it.

A wave hit it. Is that unusual?

Oh yes. At sea? Chance in a million.

So, what do you do to protect the environment in cases like this?

Well, the ship was towed outside the environment.

Into another environment.

No, no, it's been towed beyond the environment. It's not in the environment.

No, from one environment to another environment.

No, it's beyond the environment. It's not in an environment. It's been towed beyond the environment.

What's out there?

There's nothing out there.

There must be something out there.

Look. There's nothing out there. All there is is sea, and birds, and fish.

And?

And 20,000 tonnes of crude oil.

And what else?

And a fire.

And anything else?

And the part of ship that the front fell off. But there's nothing else out there.

Senator Collins, thanks for joining us.

It's a complete void.

Yes. We're out of time.

The environment is perfectly safe. We're out of time? Can you book me a cab?

But didn't you come in a Commonwealth car?

Well, yes, I did, but . . .

What happened?

The front fell off.

Interview with The Hon. John Dawkins, Minister for Education.

THE IDEA OF A UNIVERSITY

Mr Dawkins, thanks for your time.
It's a pleasure.
You're the Minister for Education, aren't you?
Yes, I am.
How long have you been Minister for Education?
I've been the Minister for about 18 months or two years.
How did it happen? Do you remember how it first happened?
I started off just being a spokesman, having a few views on education – things like the TAFEs and the primary schools, the best way to buy chalk, small things like that.
What is the best way to buy chalk?
You get it in sticks, I suppose you would call them, about four inches long.
How many would you buy at a time?
If you know where to go, I've seen people buying boxes of 20 and 30 at a time.
Could you go out of here now, say, and buy some chalk?
Yes, no trouble.
And what have you done as Minister for Education?
I've introduced a very full range of reforms right across the entire spectrum of the Australian education system and the curric . . . cccricc . . .
The curriculum?
Yes, the curricoleum.
The curriculum.
The what?
The curriculum.
Yes, that too.
What sort of reform?
What I was instructed to do by the Prime Minister and the Treasurer.
Which was what?
Get rid of the poor. I've introduced a tertiary education tax.
What is that?
It's a way of getting university students to pay for the costs involved in university education.
Aren't the universities already paid for?
Yes they are.
Aren't they funded out of taxation?
Yes, of course they are.
Haven't we already paid then?
Yes we have.

So you are asking people to pay twice?

Yes.

Will they agree to it?

They won't get into a university if they don't.

Where are you going to get the money from?

The plan is to get it out of them when they've finished their economics degrees.

So, in effect, you're blackmailing them.

Yes.

Who pays their fees in the first place?

They do.

Where do they get the money from?

Probably their parents – I don't know.

Who pays for their accommodation and living expenses and transport and books and so on?

Probably their parents.

And who are you getting into the university system?

At the moment we're getting a lot of people with fairly rich parents.

Is this a good idea?

I think so. They're able to go through university with the same people they went to school with and it helps with carpooling. There's a continuity about it.

Isn't it Labor Party policy to provide free education?

Used to be.

It used to be your policy?

No, we used to be the Labor Party.

If we could turn now to research, which is the other major function of the university system . . .

That won't change.

How will it be done?

It will be done as it is now.

Where will it be done?

It's a vital function and will continue to be done as it is now, in areas designated for research.

Where?

Oh, Japan, Taiwan, Sweden. They do a lot of it in Europe, America Spain, Poland, Brazil and Wales.

Do you get out much?

Not any more, no, I can't. It's too difficult. I've got to put the beard on, the wig, change my suit, jack up the police escort. It's just too hard.

So, what do you do?

I stay at home a lot, watch a bit of television.

Do you read?

Read? No, I don't. Wish I could.

Interview with David Hill,
Professional Bureaucrat and Freelance Genius

Mr Hill, can I ask you, have you ever produced a television programme?
Not personally, no.
Ever produced a film?
Not as such, no.
Have you ever written a film or a TV show?
No I haven't.
Did you ever design a set?
Not a set, no.
Any costumes?
Not costumes specifically.
Are you a member of Actors' Equity?
Not at the moment.
What about directing? Have you ever directed a film?
Not yet, no.
How about editing?
I've never done any editing at all.
Mixing?
What exactly is mixing?
Did you ever work in make-up?
No.
Were you ever a grip?
A grip? No.
Gaffer?
Do. I don't, thanks.
Ever worked with computer graphics?
Ironically, no.
Overseas sales?
Never heard of them.
Have you ever production-managed?
Are you looking for a yes/no answer?
Yes.
No.
Have you ever been a lighting director or cameraman?
Which one?
Either.
No.
What about sound-recording?
What about it?

Have you ever done it?
Professionally?
Yes.
No.
Non-professionally.
Sound-recording?
Yes.
No.
Have you ever worked as a film or television critic?
Not in the sense of actually doing it, no.
What is your current occupation?
I am the Chief Executive of the Australian Broadcasting Corporation.

THIS WEEK ON ABC TELEVISION
A Day-by-Day Guide to Viewing Pleasure

MONDAY

6.08 The Goodies.
Repeat of oft-repeated BBC Repeat. Repeat.
6.21 Shit Hot!
ABC Children's magazine
programme featuring whatever crap we got
off the satellite. Repeat.
**8.13 Comedy Classics: Carry On Up the
Pox.** Irreverent British Comedy. Repeat.
8.20 Upstairs Downstairs.
Repeat of repeat British drama series about
the Class System. Repeat.
9.06 Hello Sailor!
Repeat of BBC Comedy about the Class
System. With Penelope Keith. This week Mrs
Situpon's loo is blocked. Repeat.
9.30 Hyperpatheticals.
Guests Michael Shrimpton, Paddy Conroy,
Sandra Levy and David Hill are cast as
executives running a national broadcasting
organisation. Hilarious. Repeat.
10.14 The 7.30 Report. Repeat.
10.26 How's Your Father?
BBC Comedy with Penelope Keith. About the
Class System. Repeat.
11.04 Jack Pissy's Australia.
An incisive look at ourselves through the eyes
of Rostered Pom Number 4682. About the
Class System. Repeat.
11.53 Soccer.
Replay of British League matches played Sat.
9 May 1964. Repeat.

TUESDAY

6.00 The Oz Game.
Brand New Quiz show. Repeat
6.28 House Rules.
Exciting new quiz show. Pick the plot.
Featuring Jacki Weaver. Repeat.
7.00 ABC News.
Featuring Jacki Weaver. Celebrity panelists
guess the News. Coming to a Shopping
Centre near you. Repeat.
7.42 The 7.30 Report.
Fabulously successful quiz show about the
money ABC presenters can earn in
commercial radio. Features Jacki Weaver.
Repeat.
8.00 True Believers.
Drama Quiz. Actors between 45 and 70 do
impressions of dead politicians. No winners so
far. Features Jacki Weaver as Robert
Menzies. Repeat.
8.30 The Last Resort.
Weekly Management quiz. Who will resign?
Who made it? Why? Repeat.
9.25 The Satellite Tonight.
Light-hearted Fun Quiz. Richard Palfreyman
tries to guess what is going on. Repeat.
10.17 The Four Minute Mile.
Sports Quiz. English Director makes English
programme about an English runner who ran
in England. Your Question: Which well-
known Australian Broadcasting organisation
is paying for it? Repeat.
11.38 Darlings of the Gods.
Entertainment Trivia time. Vivien Leigh and
Laurence Olivier doing an off-season quick
bucks Australian tour. Vital chapter in the
searing anthem of our history etc. etc. etc.
Repeat.
**2.14 Stereo Special Simulcast Arts
Cultural Genius Masterclass.**
Some foreigner with a piano. Repeat.

WEDNESDAY

5.00 Who Farted?
ABC Children's Series.
5.30 A Little Bit of the Other.
Repeat of BBC Comedy.
6.00 How Big Was My Willie?
Repeat of BBC Comedy Series.
6.15 Grandma's Drawers. Repeat of
BBC Comedy Series.
7.00 ABC News. Repeat of earlier
bulletin on Ch 10.
7.03 Commercials.
Repeat of the 8 cents a day message and other
advertising material.
7.30 David Hill.
Portrait of a Genius. Mike Walsh profiles the
shadowy figure of ABC Supremo David Hill.
Topics will include Hill's promise not to run
British Sitcoms, his promise to produce 100
hours of Australian Drama and his famous
remarks about ratings. Repeat.
8.00 Palace of Dreams.
Repeat of fabulously interesting programme
written by Sandra Levy, Head of ABC
Drama.
9.00 The World Tonight.
Important New Flagship Current Affairs
Programme. Replaced at last minute by
Repeat of The Saturday Show; pile of old
Goat-Droppings made by Michael Shrimpton,
Head of Programmes.
9.27 Not the Vicar's Pussy.
Repeat of BBC Comedy.
9.53 Talking Shop.
An executive discusses executive decision-
making with another executive who discusses
it with Hill. Hill makes a few phone calls and
gets back to the second executive about what
the first executive should say.
12.00 Four Corners.
Modified TV Version.
12.02 Edge of Darkness.
[Times subject to change without notice]
1.30 The Singing Detective.
2.16 Close.

THURSDAY

• Viewers are advised that in an attempt to
increase the size of its audience, the ABC will
not be broadcasting its advertised programmes
tonight. A videotape of management
explaining what went wrong and photographs
of the $600 million will be available through
ABC Marketing as soon as they get back from
long service leave. The following programmes
can be seen on SBS:28 UHF.
3.30 Piff Paff Poff.
5.30 Bing Bang Bong.
6.00 Klop Klop Klop.
6.30 World News.
7.00 Sports Report.
7.30 Books.
Dinny O'Hearn speaks to McPhee about the
influence of Brian Johns on Gribble.
8.00 Nei Bis.
Japanese Drama Serial.
8.30 Probe.
Susan Ryan talks to Brian Gribble about
Dinny McPhee's book of poems.
9.00 Dark Madness.
German/Polish drama. A young woman
process worker analyses her own suicide.
10.15 Talking Publishing.
Hilary O'Hearn presents a discussion with
Susan Johns about Brian McPhee's new
novel 'Gribble'.
10.40 The Movie Show.
Featuring Margaret and David. Cleverly-
crafted psycho-drama about the partners in
an up-market bughouse tormenting one
another.
11.20 Showbiz.
Presented by Buffoona. A roundup of new
discos.
11.50 Soccer.
Match between Das Pomeranzski and Il
Strattoni played 29.5.88.

FRIDAY

6.02 The World at Six.
Satellite stories shown previously on commercial stations. Part of the commitment to excellence in investigative journalism. Repeat.

6.33 House Rules.
Possibly a drama programme. Part of commitment to avoid mindless quest for ratings. Repeat.

7.02 News. Includes Sport, Weather, Recipes, Shopping Hints, Haircare, Promos for other programmes and Panda Corner. Repeat.

7.36 The 7.30 Report.
Exclusive interview with Freddie and the Dreamers. Ground breaking current affairs initiative. Repeat.

8.07 You Bloody Ripper Bottler Ball-Tearer Tucker Man. Repeat.

8.39 Open All Hours.
Top quality antique trouser-jokes in agreeably working-class accents. Starring Ronnie Barker as Arnold Bollocks. Part of the commitment to 100 hours of Australian Drama per year. Repeat.

9.13 The Last Resort.
Curiously haunting indictment of ABC Drama Dept. Repeat.

10.26 The World at 10.03.
Pushing out the frontiers of News Gathering. Discussion about UFOs. Repeat.

10.54 Rugby.
Replay of match between East Grinstead and Swansea, played 19 April 43BC. Repeat.

11.42 Close. Repeat.
'Advance Australia Fair' is played this evening by the Bendigo Fire Brigade Band and sung by the Ballarat Choristers. Copies available from ABC Marketing.

SATURDAY

4.51 Weekend News.
Preview of the 7.00 News which was run at 6.00 weekends but now moved to 5.15 Saturday and 4.36 Sunday [12.00 Adelaide] except during Lent or following Football replay to the state where the match broadcast is not being played. Repeat.

6.23 Touch The Sun.
Children's Series. The most expensive programme ever made. Eight government bodies fund each other to produce film about a blue-healer who saves Kakadu. Repeat.

7.31 The Last Resort.
ABC Drama Series. Tonight Narelle and Joylene Chekhov are approached by a left-handed Nepalese Plumber whose mother has just crossed the Atlantic on a marital requisite. Delwyn Chekhov discovers a cure for Surfing. Starring some people someone met at a party. Repeat.

8.03 Clive Hale Shouts Backwards at the Audience. Repeat.

8.56 Clanger.
ABC Drama Co-production. Boring man in raincoat driven around Sydney until the budget is used up. Repeat.

9.24 Gawd Luvvaduck!
Repeat BBC Comedy Series. Repeat.

9.58 The Yeldham Years.
Story of the man who rode around Australia saying 'Have you heard about this Sarajevo business? Some Bosnian student shot the Austrian King's nephew. Shagger and I have joined up. Ethel doesn't mind. Reckons it's our duty. Could be the end of the Old World but' Repeat.

10.17 A Turn for the Nurse.
Repeat BBC Comedy Series. Repeat.

10.41 The World the Night before Last.
Crack ABC Recent Affairs Programme. Repeat.

10.74 Not On Your Nellie!
Repeat BBC Comedy Series. Repeat.

11.25 Close. Repeat.
[Times may vary.]

SUNDAY

5.00 The World at 5.
Roundup of news stories from previous
weeks. Repeat.
5.27 The World at 5.30. Repeat.
6.09 The World at 6. Repeat.
6.36 The World at 6.30. Repeat.
7.04 The World at 7. Repeat.
7.38 The World at 7.30. Repeat.
8.44 The World at 8. Repeat.
9.12 The World at 9.12. Repeat.
9.56 The World at 5 to 10. Repeat.
10.29 The World at 9.30. Repeat.
10.57 The World at 1/4 to 3. Repeat.
11.20 The World at 20 past 6. Repeat.
11.63 The World at half past 2. Repeat.
12.98 Close. Repeat.

• Viewers are advised that due to an
industrial dispute the advertised programmes
will not be broadcast tonight.

Viewers wishing to support this policy should
contact:

The David Hill Personal
Publicity Organisation
The Academy de Tap,
Glamour Photography House,
Sydney 2000 NSW.

Stop Press

Transcript of the announcement made last night following the Possibles v Probables match played at Eden Park. The Chairman of the New Zealand Rugby Football Union, Mr Richie Guy.

"The following is the All Black team chosen to represent New Zealand in the World Cup to be played in Europe commencing on 3 October.

Fullback	E.P. Hillary, Auckland
Wing Three-quarters	R.L. Hall, Otago
	G.C. Sydney, Otago
Centre	K.J. Te Kanawa, Auckland
Second Five-eight	S. Neill, Otago
First Five-eight	A. Curnow, Auckland
Halfback	R. Hotere, Otago
Number Eight	H. Morrison, Auckland
Flankers	L. Tamahori, Wellington
	J. Campion, Wellington
Locks	B.T. Finn, King Country
	N.M. Finn, King Country
Props	K. Hulme, West Coast
	J.P. Frame, Otago
Hooker	M. Mahy, Canterbury
Reserves	P. Jackson, Wellington
	R.J. McWhannell, Auckland
	R. O'Brien, Taranaki
	M. Urlich, Auckland
	S. O'Neill, Marlborough
	J. Lill, Auckland
	D. Dobbyn, Auckland
	J. Morris, Wellington
Captain	E.P. Hillary
Masseur	J. Rowles
Manager	Mr J.P. Hanly

Following the Announcement We Spoke to Ex-All Black and Current Selector Owen Higgins.

If I could just take you through this side, Owen.

Yes certainly. We think it's a very good side, obviously. There are always disappointments but we think it's a balanced side. This will be a tough campaign and what we were looking for was a side with experience and discipline but a side that wouldn't be frightened to throw the ball around if the opportunity presents itself.

Yes, I wonder if we could just go through it. You've obviously gone for experience at fullback.

Yes. That's where a lot of the pressure is going to be, of course, the high up and under, and I think it's going to make everyone feel better just knowing Ed's back there.

Will he come up into the line?

Well, he certainly can and it would be a mistake for the opposition to assume he won't if he gets an opportunity.

It's been a feature of his game over many years, of course.

It has. It's been a great strength for him, yes.

He's deceptive, isn't he?

He is a very deceptive mover. He's a big fellow and you don't always think he's moving too rapidly but you try and bring him down.

He's always just got that burst of acceleration.

He has.

How's his kicking?

Oh, very solid.

You've got an awful lot of experience on the wings, as well,

Yes, we have.

Although Hall hasn't played a lot this year, has he?

He missed the first part of the season with a corked thigh but he played very well against the Welsh. He'll have a fitness test but I'd expect him to play.

One of the great tacticians of the game.

Oh, he never stops thinking, Roger.

Sydney on the other wing.

Yes, you can never leave Grahame out of a side. The try he scored against the French last year was an absolute pearler.

It was a beauty, wasn't it?

It was one of the great things I've ever witnessed.

Lost a yard or two of his pace since then, though, don't you think?

Well, I don't know whether you saw him in the trials but he went through some pretty serious midfield defence a couple of times as if there was nobody home.

Centre.

Kiri. Yes, what can I say.

Completely dominates, doesn't she.

Oh. Just so strong. Must be a dream to play outside.

Yes, good ball and you'd get it running.

And she doesn't mind tackling.

She wraps up a lot of very dangerous players, doesn't she.

She can stop an attack stone dead.

You've got Neill at second-five.

Yes, we've wasted a lot of ball in that area in the last couple of years and Sam's got a wonderful ability to straighten things up. He passes well and he can take a tackle without losing the ball and the ABs do alright out of the secondary phase stuff.

He can carve up a defence, too, mind you.

My very word he can. He stands very deep and he takes the ball running and he makes an awful hole if he gets through.

Curnow.

Hands. Beautiful hands.

He has got beautiful hands.

And feet.

Yes, lovely pair of feet, too.

Hands and feet.

What more could you want?

And a brain.

A great football brain. He's always there, Allen. He's one of those people. He's back in defence, he's up in attack.

He's everywhere.

He's everywhere. There aren't many places he isn't.

He's played a lot of his football outside Hotere.

He has. And Ralph's played a lot of his football inside Allen, of course. I don't know how Hotere knows where his backs are half the time but you can

often see him in the middle of a pile of players and you think "How can he possibly get the the ball out of there?" and then a long pass comes out of nowhere and finds Curnow.

It's miraculous.

It is. He's a running halfback too, of course, Ralph.

He is. He is. Perhaps a bit of Sid Going in there.

He had a problem with a hip, didn't he?

He had an operation, yes, for a pinched nerve but I don't know whether you saw him on Saturday.

Yes, I did.

Not much evidence of pinched nerves there.

No. He seems to love playing with Howard Morrison too, doesn't he?

They do have some sort of understanding, yes. Howard will sometimes hold the ball in the back of the maul and then detach himself and feed Ralph.

Yes, they did that a lot against Scotland.

They did. It works particularly well when you're trying to create room on the blind side because it forces the defence to run very wide. Howard does it beautifully off the back of the lineouts as well.

This Lee Tamahori is incredibly quick, isn't he? Did you know he was that fast? He was all over the inside backs like a blanket on Saturday.

He's incredibly fast and he's very much a form player right now. Right now Lee is playing some of the best rugby you'll see anywhere.

He and Jane work well together, don't they?

Yes, very much so. They've improved the New Zealand defence probably 100 per cent. Nothing gets past them. Although, of course, they're also a very attacking combination. How Jane got out to pick up Te Kanawa's pass against England I'll never know.

Yes, what was she doing out there?

I don't know. She made two hits when the English were driving forward, the ABs turned it over and Sam stood his man up for Kiri to go through and she said she couldn't believe it. Roger was outside her but he was tackled without the ball and she heard Jane calling for the pass inside so she just flicked it in and there she was.

Goodnight nurse.

Gone.

47-3.

Yes, sealed the match, I suppose.

We were quietly confident at that point, yes.

Yes.

The Finn brothers locking the scrum.

Yes. There must be something in the water up there. There have been a few good combinations from up that way.

Wasn't there an injury cloud there with Tim?

There was at one stage, yes, but he's over that now.

He looked very good the other day.

He's a very fit boy.

Now, the front row. This is one of the great front rows in world rugby, isn't it?

I don't think the game has seen a better front row than this.

Kerry Hulme tight-head.

What can you say about Kerry. It doesn't matter what they throw up against her, she just gets better.

Did you see her laughing when she scored a try in the trials?

Yes. I don't think she expects to get a lot of tries. She would have just loved it. Apparently she was asking people afterwards how many tries they'd scored.

And Janet Frame on the other side.

Yes, it's not a bad engineroom is it? There's more experience in that front row than anywhere else, including the stand. Janet has toured every major rugby playing nation, she's played on every ground, there's nothing that's going to phase Janet. And, of course, she's great with anyone just coming into the national side.

And Margaret Mahy.

Yes, a hooker who can kick goals. How often do you see that?

Has anyone got more scrums against the head anywhere in the world?

No, although she says that's more to do with Kerry and Janet.

What do they say?

They say whatever they like.

Margaret and Ralph Hotere are the team comedians, of course, aren't they?

Oh yes, very lively customers the pair of them,

On the bus, I mean.

Yes I think it's fair to say they'd be leading the festivities. It should be a good tour.

Yes. We're all looking forward to it.
Oh yes, it should be terrific,
Well good luck.
Thanks.
And please convey all of our very best wishes to the team.
I most certainly will.
Thanks again for coming in.
That's a pleasure.
Thanks for your time.
No trouble.
Thanks.
Thank you.
And good luck with the tour. Thank you.
Yes. Thanks.
I've been talking to Owen Higgins. Back to you Keith.